First World War
and Army of Occupation
War Diary
France, Belgium and Germany

52 DIVISION
Headquarters, Branches and Services
Royal Army Medical Corps
Assistant Director Medical Services
1 April 1918 - 30 June 1919

WO95/2891/1

The Naval & Military Press Ltd
www.nmarchive.com
Published in association with The National Archives

Published by

The Naval & Military Press Ltd

Unit 10 Ridgewood Industrial Park,

Uckfield, East Sussex,

TN22 5QE England

Tel: +44 (0) 1825 749494

www.naval-military-press.com

www.nmarchive.com

This diary has been reprinted in facsimile from the original. Any imperfections are inevitably reproduced and the quality may fall short of modern type and cartographic standards.

Contents

Document type	Place/Title	Date From	Date To
Heading	WO95/2891/1 Assistant Director Medical Services		
Heading	52nd Division Asst Dir. Medical Services 1918 Apl-1919 Jun		
Heading	A.D.M.S. 52nd Div 17th-30th April 1918		
Heading	War Diary Of A.D.M.S. 52nd Division 1st April To 30th April 1918 Volume 4		
War Diary	Jaffa	01/04/1918	02/04/1918
War Diary	Surafend	03/04/1918	07/04/1918
War Diary	Alexandria	09/04/1918	11/04/1918
War Diary	Marseilles	17/04/1918	17/04/1918
War Diary	Rue Near Abbeville	20/04/1918	23/04/1918
War Diary	Rue	24/04/1918	28/04/1918
War Diary	Aire	29/04/1918	30/04/1918
Heading	A.D.M.S. 52nd Div. May 1918		
Heading	War Diary Of A.D.M.S. 52nd Division From 1st To 31st May 1918 (Volume 5)		
War Diary	Aire	01/05/1918	06/05/1918
War Diary	Villers Au Bois	06/05/1918	06/05/1918
War Diary	Chateau D'Acq	07/05/1918	07/05/1918
War Diary	Villers Au Bois	07/05/1918	07/05/1918
War Diary	Chateau D'Acq	07/05/1918	31/05/1918
Operation(al) Order(s)	R.A.M.C. Operation Order No. 1 by Col A.J. MacDougall A.M.S. A.D.M.S 52nd Division	04/05/1918	04/05/1918
Miscellaneous	Transport And Mounted Personnel March Table	05/05/1918	05/05/1918
Operation(al) Order(s)	R.A.M.C. Operation Order No. 2 by Col A.J. MacDougall A.M.S. A.D.M.S 52nd Division	05/05/1918	05/05/1918
Miscellaneous	Reference 62nd Division Order No. 195	13/05/1918	13/05/1918
Miscellaneous	Ammendments to Medical Arrangements In The Event Of Active Operations	17/05/1918	17/05/1918
Miscellaneous	Medical Arrangements No.2 52nd (Lowland) Division	17/05/1918	17/05/1918
Miscellaneous	Medical Arrangements In The Event Of Active Operations	17/05/1918	17/05/1918
Miscellaneous	R.A.M.C. Operation Order No. 3 By A.D.M.S. 52nd (London) Division	23/05/1918	23/05/1918
Miscellaneous	Medical Arrangements No.3	27/05/1918	27/05/1918
Heading	War Diary Of A.D.M.S. 52nd Division From 1st To 30th June 1918 (Volume 6)		
War Diary	Chateau D'Acq	01/06/1918	30/06/1918
Miscellaneous	A.D.M.S. 52nd Divn. No.948/4.	18/06/1918	18/06/1918
Heading	War Diary Of A.D.M.S. 52nd Divn. From 1st July To 31st July 1918. (Volume 7)		
War Diary	Chateau D'Acq	01/07/1918	23/07/1918
War Diary	Pernes	23/07/1918	31/07/1918
Miscellaneous	Summary Of Medical Arrangements 52nd (Lowland) Division.	04/07/1918	04/07/1918
Miscellaneous	Addendum To Medical Arrangements In The Event Of A Hostile Attack-52nd Division	04/07/1918	04/07/1918
Miscellaneous	Medical Arrangements		
Miscellaneous	Appendix II		
Operation(al) Order(s)	R.A.M.C. Operation Order No. 6	21/07/1918	21/07/1918

Miscellaneous	Medical Arrangements For 157 Brigade Group	20/07/1918	20/07/1918
Operation(al) Order(s)	R.A.M.C. Operation Order No. 7. By Lieut Colonel J.W. Leitch D.S.O.	30/07/1918	30/07/1918
Miscellaneous	Amendment To R.A.M.C. Operation Order No. 7	30/07/1918	30/07/1918
Heading	War Diary Of A.D.M.S. 52nd Division 1st To 31st August 1918 (Volume 8)		
War Diary	Pernes	01/08/1918	01/08/1918
War Diary	Maroeuil	02/08/1918	16/08/1918
War Diary	Villers Chatel	17/08/1918	21/08/1918
War Diary	Hermaville	22/08/1918	22/08/1918
War Diary	Bretencourt	23/08/1918	23/08/1918
War Diary	Blairville	24/08/1918	31/08/1918
Operation(al) Order(s)	R.A.M.C. Operation Order No. 8 by Col A.J. MacDougall A.M.S. A.D.M.S 52nd (Lowland) Division	15/08/1918	15/08/1918
Operation(al) Order(s)	R.A.M.C. Operation Order No. 10 by Col A.J. MacDougall A.M.S. A.D.M.S 52nd (Lowland) Divn	23/08/1918	23/08/1918
Operation(al) Order(s)	R.A.M.C. Operation Order No. 12 by Col A.J. MacDougall A.M.S. A.D.M.S 52nd (Lowland) Divn	25/08/1918	25/08/1918
Operation(al) Order(s)	R.A.M.C. Operation Order No. 13 by Col A.J. MacDougall A.M.S. A.D.M.S 52nd (Lowland) Divn	27/08/1918	27/08/1918
Operation(al) Order(s)	R.A.M.C. Operation Order No. 14 by A.D.M.S 52nd (Lowland) Division	30/08/1918	30/08/1918
Heading	War Diary Of A.D.M.S. 52nd Division Sept 1st To Sept 31st 1918 Volume 9		
War Diary	Map 51B S.W.	01/09/1918	16/09/1918
War Diary	Queant	17/09/1918	30/09/1918
Operation(al) Order(s)	R.A.M.C. Operation Order No. 15 by A.D.M.S 52nd (Lowland) Division	01/09/1918	01/09/1918
Operation(al) Order(s)	R.A.M.C. Operation Order No. 17 by A.D.M.S 52nd (Lowland) Division	14/09/1918	14/09/1918
Operation(al) Order(s)	R.A.M.C. Operation Order No. 18 by A.D.M.S 52nd (Lowland) Division	25/09/1918	25/09/1918
Operation(al) Order(s)	R.A.M.C. Operation Order No. 19 by A.D.M.S 52nd (Lowland) Division	01/10/1918	01/10/1918
Heading	A.D.M.S. 52nd Division War Diary-October 1918 Volume X		
War Diary	Graincourt	01/10/1918	22/10/1918
War Diary	Blanche Maison	23/10/1918	23/10/1918
War Diary	Flers	24/10/1918	28/10/1918
War Diary	Sameon	29/10/1918	31/10/1918
Operation(al) Order(s)	R.A.M.C. Operation Order No. 20 by A.D.M.S 52nd Division	18/10/1918	18/10/1918
Operation(al) Order(s)	R.A.M.C. Operation Order No. 21 by A.D.M.S 52nd (Lowland) Division	27/10/1918	27/10/1918
Heading	War Diary Of A.D.M.S. 52nd (Lowland) Division From 1st Novr To 30th Novr 1918. (Volume XI)		
War Diary	Sameon	01/11/1918	27/11/1918
War Diary	Nimy	28/11/1918	30/11/1918
Operation(al) Order(s)	R.A.M.C. Operation Order No. 22 by A.D.M.S 52nd (Lowland) Division	04/11/1918	04/11/1918
Operation(al) Order(s)	R.A.M.C. Operation Order No. 24 by A.D.M.S 52nd (Lowland) Division	08/11/1918	08/11/1918
Heading	War Diary of A.D.M.S. 52nd Division From 1st To 31st December 1918 (Volume 12)		
War Diary	Nimy	01/12/1918	31/12/1918

Miscellaneous	A.D.M.S. 52nd Divn. No. R.828/2.	09/12/1918	09/12/1918
Heading	War Diary Of A.D.M.S. 52nd Division From 1st To 31st January 1919 (Volume 1)		
War Diary		01/01/1919	31/01/1919
Heading	War Diary Of A.D.M.S. 52nd Division From 1st To 28th Feby 1919 (Volume 2)		
War Diary		01/02/1919	28/02/1919
Miscellaneous	Notice. Appendix No.1 Sheet 7		
Heading	War Diary Of A.D.M.S. 52nd Division From 1st March To 31st March 1919 (Volume 2)		
War Diary	Nimy Near Mons. Belgium	01/03/1919	24/03/1919
War Diary	Soignies	25/03/1919	31/03/1919
Miscellaneous	Appendix 1		
Miscellaneous	Appendix II	14/02/1919	14/02/1919
Miscellaneous	Appendix III	11/03/1919	11/03/1919
Heading	War Diary Of A.D.M.S. 52nd (Lowland) Division From 1st April 1919 To 30th April 1919 (Volume 13)		
War Diary	Soignies	01/04/1919	01/04/1919
War Diary	Belgium	02/04/1919	07/04/1919
War Diary	Soignies	07/04/1919	31/05/1919
Miscellaneous	Central Registry		
Heading	War Diary June 1919 A.D.M.S. 52 Lowland Division.		
War Diary	Ohligs	01/06/1919	30/06/1919
Miscellaneous	Lowland Division Medical Arrangements No 3 App I	17/06/1919	17/06/1919

WO95/2891/1

Assistant Director Medical Services

52ND DIVISION

ASST DIR.MEDICAL SERVICES

~~APR. - DEC 1918~~

1918 APL - 1919 JUN

1st – 30th April 1918

A.D.M.S. 52nd Div

Confidential

War Diary

of

A.D.M.S. 52nd Division

1st April to 30th April 1918

VOLUME 4

E.E.F.

Instructions regarding War Diaries and Intelligence Summaries are contained in F. S. Regs., Part II. and the Staff Manual respectively. Title pages will be prepared in manuscript.

WAR DIARY
or
~~INTELLIGENCE SUMMARY.~~
(Erase heading not required.)

Army Form C. 2118.

A.D.M.S. 52 Div
April 1918

1

Place	Date	Hour	Summary of Events and Information	Remarks and references to Appendices
JAFFA	1.4.18		52 Divisional Sanitary Section marched to SURAFEND	[illegible]
			3 Lowland Fld Ambulance left SARONA for SURAFEND at 1830.	
	2.4.18		Headquarters 52 Div left JAFFA for SURAFEND near LUDD	[illegible]
SURAFEND	3.4.18		Visited D.M.S. Inquired as to disposal of Divisional Dental Surgeon on Division moving to France; and as to OC Sanitary Section who has been ordered to report to A.D.M.S. Force in Egypt but whose successor is in hospital at present	[illegible]
			Ordered Division Dental Surgeon to report to A.D.M.S. 53 Div & to return his equipment to A. Depot Med. Stores at LUDD	
	4.5.18		1st Lowland Fld Ambulance with 156 Brigade entrained at LUDD last night for embarkation at ALEXANDRIA	
			2nd Lowland Field Ambulance left SARONA last night & arrived at SURAFEND this morning	

D. D. & L., London, E.C.
(A8001) Wt. W1271/M2031 750,000 5/17 Sch. 52 Forms/C2118/14

Instructions regarding War Diaries and Intelligence Summaries are contained in F. S. Regs., Part II. and the Staff Manual respectively. Title pages will be prepared in manuscript.

WAR DIARY
or
INTELLIGENCE SUMMARY.
(Erase heading not required.)

Army Form C. 2118.

ADMS. 52 Div

APRIL 1918

2

Place	Date	Hour	Summary of Events and Information	Remarks and references to Appendices
SURAFEND	5 IV 18		Capt P STEWART RAMC att 5 HLI ordered to report to A.D.MS 54 Div, his place being taken by Lieut MACKENZIE from that Division.	[initials]
			3 Lowland Fld Ambulance with 155 Brigade entrained last night at LUDD with it was the 52 Sanitary Section ~~[illegible]~~ The Sanitary Section is at present attached to the ambulance as no officer has at present come to take over from Capt PIERCE who has been ordered to report to A.D.MS Forces in Egypt.	
"	6 IV 18		Received intimation that Capt GREER RAMC had been ordered to report for duty with 3 Lowland Fld Ambulance	[initials]
"	7 IV 18		Divisional Headquarters entrained at LUDD last night	
			2nd Lowland Fld ambulance with 157 Brigade entrained at LUDD last night	[initials]

D. D. & L., London, E.C. (A6001) Wt. W1 71/M2031 750,000 5/17 Sch. 52 Forms/C2118/14

Instructions regarding War Diaries and Intelligence Summaries are contained in F. S. Regs., Part II. and the Staff Manual respectively. Title pages will be prepared in manuscript.

WAR DIARY
or
INTELLIGENCE SUMMARY.
(Erase heading not required.)

Army Form C. 2118.

ADMS 52 Div
APRIL 1918

13

Place	Date	Hour	Summary of Events and Information	Remarks and references to Appendices
ALEXANDRIA	9.IV.18		On arrival at ALEXANDRIA Divisional Headquarters embarked on H.T. INDARRA + the other medical units of the Division are distributed as follows	
			1st Lowland FA on the CANBERRA & LEASOWE CASTLE	
			2nd " " INDARRA, OMRAH & CALEDONIA	
			3rd " " KAISER I. HIND & MALWA &	
			52 Sanitary Section on MALWA	
			Capt MURRY reported for duty as OC Sanitary Co.	
			Lieut Col DUNNING under orders from GHQ reported to proceed with 2 Lowland Fld Ambulance	
			As Lieut Col Dunning left this ambulance about 2 months ago & Major BURNS was posted to command it, I wired to D.M.S. asking whether Lieut Col DUNNING was to supersede Major BURNS in command or whether Major BURNS was to retain command, the answer received was that Lt Col Dunning was to take over command	

D. D. & L., London, E.C. (A6001) Wt. W1 71/M2031 750,000 5/17 Sch. 52 Forms/C2118/14

Instructions regarding War Diaries and Intelligence Summaries are contained in F. S. Regs., Part II. and the Staff Manual respectively. Title pages will be prepared in manuscript.

WAR DIARY
or
INTELLIGENCE SUMMARY.
(Erase heading not required.)

[Arm]y Form C. 2118.

A.D.M.S. [illegible] April 1918 4

Place	Date	Hour	Summary of Events and Information	Remarks and references to Appendices
ALEXANDRIA	11.IV.18		Convoy set out from ALEXANDRIA about 1630 today	[initials]
MARSE[ILLES]	17 IV 18		Convoy arrived at MARSEILLES this morning. Divisional Headquarte[rs] disembarked & entrained, at 2147 leaving for an unknown destination	
RUE near ABBEVILLE	20 IV 18		Divisional Headquarters disentrained at NOYELLES SUR MER & marched to RUE in the neighbourhood of which the division is to be billeted	[initials]
	21 IV 18		1 Lowland Fld ambulance arrived & was billeted in RUE	
	22 IV 18		3 Lowland Fld Ambulance & billeted at ARRY.	
			Visited the 156 Brigade in neighbourhood of ST FIRMIN & ST QUENTIN.	
			On 20.IV.18 reported my arrival to D.M.S. Reserve Army	
	23 IV 18		1st & 3 Lowland Fld ambulances directed to draw vehicles horses & harness today.	

D. D. & L., London, E.C.
(A8001) Wt. W1 71/M2031 750,000 5/17 Sch. 52 Forms/C2118/14

Instructions regarding War Diaries and Intelligence Summaries are contained in F. S. Regs., Part II. and the Staff Manual respectively. Title pages will be prepared in manuscript.

WAR DIARY
or
~~INTELLIGENCE SUMMARY.~~
(Erase heading not required.)

A.D.M.S. 52 Div
April

Form C. 2118.

5

Place	Date	Hour	Summary of Events and Information	Remarks and references to Appendices
RUE	24.IV.18		M.O. 4 R.S.F. reported 4 cases of Scarlet fever in his battalion. Cases have been sent to hospital & contacts isolated. The 4 cases occurred in 2 tents 2 in each & were probably infected either in Camp MONTFURON MARSELLES or in the train from MARSEILLES to NOYELLES.	CW
			2 Lowland Field Ambulance directed to draw horses & vehicles today.	
"	25 IV.18		Recommended that 4 R.S.F. be kept in the camp in which they are not moved into billets as proposed that the Machine gun battalion also be kept with them. Another case has occurred & all contacts 27 in number in 3 tents have been isolated the tents disinfected & separate latrine accommodation supplied for contacts	CW
"	26 IV.18		Orders issued for billeting parties of ambulances to leave by lorry tomorrow morning	

D. D. & L., London, E.C.
(A8001) Wt. W1 71/M2031 750,000 5/17 Sch. 52 Forms/C2118/14

Form C. 2118.

WAR DIARY
or
~~INTELLIGENCE SUMMARY.~~
(*Erase heading not required.*)

- Instructions regarding War Diaries and Intelligence Summaries are contained in F. S. Regs., Part II. and the Staff Manual respectively. Title pages will be prepared in manuscript.

ADMS 52 Div
APRIL 1918

6

Place	Date	Hour	Summary of Events and Information	Remarks and references to Appendices
RUE	26.IV.18		Recommended that machine gun battalion & 4 S Fus. do not move with battalion, but remain in present camp for 10 days from last case of Scarlet fever occurs.	[illegible]
	27.IV.18		Went to AIRE to see DDMS XI Corps 1st ARMY under whom the division is coming returning after seeing him.	[illegible]
	28.IV.18		Headquarter Division less advanced parties entrained at RUE at 1744.	
			1 Lowland Fld ambulance left RUE at 1900.	
AIRE	29.IV.18		Arrived at AIRE. Hdquarters in RUE ST OMER	[illegible]
			The remainder of division entraining today at NOYELLES & RUE except the Artillery Machine gun battalion & 4 RSF who are remaining & the 156 Brigade who came on in advance	
	30.IV.18		The 1/2 Lowland Fld & 1/3 Lowland FA arrived this morning.	

D. D. & L., London, E.C. (A8004) Wt. W1-71/M2031 750,000 5/17 Sch. 52 Forms/C2118/14

Instructions regarding War Diaries and Intelligence Summaries are contained in F. S. Regs., Part II. and the Staff Manual respectively. Title pages will be prepared in manuscript.

WAR DIARY
or
INTELLIGENCE SUMMARY.
(Erase heading not required.)

Form C. 2118.

ADMS. 62 Div 7

APRIL

Place	Date	Hour	Summary of Events and Information	Remarks and references to Appendices
AIRE	30.IV.18		Visited Fld ambulances who are located as follows: 1/1 Lowland Fld ambulance Les TOURBIERES 1/2 " " " La LACQUE Camp 1/3 " " " COHEM The accommodation of each Field Ambulance is meagre being in small houses in villages except the 1/2 F.A who are in huts in the camp which is crowded. The other units of the Division are in AIRE, La LACQUE Camp & surrounding villages. [signature] Col ADMS	

D. D. & L., London, E.C. (A8001) Wt. W1771/M2031 750,000 5/17 Sch. 52 Forms/C2118/14

May 1918

140/2973

A. D. M. S. 52nd Div.

Confidential

War Diary
of
A.D.M.S. 52ND DIVISION.

FROM 1ST TO 31ST MAY. 1918.

(VOLUME. 5.)

Vol. 2

Army Form C. 2118.

Instructions regarding War Diaries and Intelligence Summaries are contained in F. S. Regs., Part II. and the Staff Manual respectively. Title pages will be prepared in manuscript.

WAR DIARY
or
INTELLIGENCE SUMMARY.
(Erase heading not required.)

A.D.M.S. 62 Div
MAY 1918

1

Place	Date	Hour	Summary of Events and Information	Remarks and references to Appendices
AIRE	1 V 18		Visited 156 Brigade units in neighbourhood of MAMETZ & inspected sanitation of units with officer of Brigade Staff. The sanitation is very crude & there is a lack of flyproof covers to latrines. wrote to Division on the subject	[illegible]
	2 V 18		Visited La LACQUE camp & the baths situated there. The 157 Brigade situated at La LACQUE is being bathed & issued with fresh clothing	[illegible]
	3 V 18		Visited the French Barracks at AIRE where certain units of the Division are billeted. Place very insanitary.	[illegible]
	4 V 18		Visited units of 186 Brigade round COHEM Visited THIENNES with a view of forming ADS between the CANAL DE LYS & FORÊT DE NIEPPE	[illegible]

D. D. & L., London, E.C.
(A8003) Wt. W1-71/M2031 750,000 5/17 Sch. 52 Forms/C2118/14

Instructions regarding War Diaries and Intelligence Summaries are contained in F. S. Regs., Part II. and the Staff Manual respectively. Title pages will be prepared in manuscript.

WAR DIARY
or
INTELLIGENCE SUMMARY.
(Erase heading not required.)

ADMS. 52 Div. May 1918. 2

Army Form C. 2118.

Place	Date	Hour	Summary of Events and Information	Remarks and references to Appendices
AIRE	5.V.18		Went to NEUVILLE ST VAAST near ARRAS & saw ADMS 4 Canadian Division. This Division is taking over the line of the left battalion of the 4 Canadian Division. The ADMS explained to me the disposition of his ambulances & regimental aid post, & shewed me the Main Dressing Station at AUX RIETZ which this Division is taking over & one Advanced Dressing station.	[initials]
			Visited the DDMS XVIII Corps into which Corps this division is coming.	
AIRE	6.V.18		Left AIRE at 11.30 today & arrived at new divisional Hdqts at CHATEAU D'ACQ about $\frac{3}{4}$ mile SW of VILLERS AU BOIS	[initials] See APPENDIX No I
VILLERS AU BOIS.			2 Lowland Fld Ambulance arrived by train & were billeted near the Main Dressing Station AUX RIETZ which they will take over, the transport arrived the same day having left AIRE	

D. D. & L., London, E.C. (A8001) Wt. W1 71/M2031 750,000 5/17 Sch. 52 Forms/C2118/14

Instructions regarding War Diaries and Intelligence Summaries are contained in F. S. Regs., Part II. and the Staff Manual respectively. Title pages will be prepared in manuscript.

WAR DIARY
or
INTELLIGENCE SUMMARY.
(Erase heading not required.)

Army Form C. 2118.

A.D.M.S. 52 Div
May 1918
3

Place	Date	Hour	Summary of Events and Information	Remarks and references to Appendices
CHATEAU D'ACQ VILLERS AU BOIS	7.V.18.		on 5.5.18. Attended conference at D.D.M.S XVIII Corps subject arrangements for treating gas cases in large numbers.	[initials]
			1/3 Lowland Field Ambulance came into St ELOI & were given a site with huts on it for Main Dressing Station, they are to have a site for A.D.S. near AU RIETZ when available	
			157 Brigade relieved 11th Canadian Brigade in left Sector of 4 Canadian Division	
			2 Lowland FA relieved 12 Canadian F.A. & took over MDS at AUX RIETZ A 8 c ADS at CHAUDERIE S18 c 93 & VIMY VILLIAGE T 25 d 94. Regimental aid posts at T8 c 95 T16 c 69 & relay posts at T12 b 78 T20 b 27 T26 a 39. The Main Dressing Station consists of 5 huts for patients with annexes & the	

D. D. & L., London, E.C.
(A8001) Wt. W1 71/M2031 750,000 5/17 Sch. 52 Forms/C2118/14

Instructions regarding War Diaries and Intelligence Summaries are contained in F. S. Regs., Part II. and the Staff Manual respectively. Title pages will be prepared in manuscript.

WAR DIARY
or
INTELLIGENCE SUMMARY.
(Erase heading not required.)

ADMS 52 Div
May 1918

Army Form C. 2118.

Place	Date	Hour	Summary of Events and Information	Remarks and references to Appendices
CHATEAU D'ACQ	7-V-18		ADS are dugouts that at CHAUDERIE being a deep German dugout that can accommodate 60 men that of VIMY being smaller.	
	8 V-18		1/1 Lowland FA arrived from AIRE & ~~[illegible]~~ is billeted at VILLER AU BOIS where it is proposed that it should form a Divisional Rest station.	
			The 155 Inf Brigade took over from the 51st Division tonight 8/9. An additional RAP T28 c 4 9 was taken over by 2 Lowland Field Ambulance, the ADS mentioned above being used for evacuation of the new area.	
	9-V-18		Attended a conference at office of DDMS on medical arrangements in case of an attack by the enemy. Proposed to evacuated walking wounded cases from AUX RIET MDS by light railway to SAVY, Stretcher cases by MAC to CCS at AUBIGNY	

D. D. & L., London, E.C.
(A8001) Wt. W1-71/M2031 750,000 5/17 Sch. 52 Forms/C2118/14

Instructions regarding War Diaries and Intelligence Summaries are contained in F. S. Regs., Part II. and the Staff Manual respectively. Title pages will be prepared in manuscript.

WAR DIARY
or
~~INTELLIGENCE SUMMARY.~~
(Erase heading not required.)

Army Form C. 2118.

A.D.M.S. 52 Div

5

Place	Date	Hour	Summary of Events and Information	Remarks and references to Appendices
CHATEAU D'ACQ	11.V.18		Visited 2 Lowland Fld Ambulance + ADS of 3 Lowland FA. Interviewed Railway Control officer at TERRITORIAL DUMP with regard to service of trains of walking wounded to SAVY referred me to control officer BOIS DE BRAY as he only dealt with traffic forward. Latter officer referred me to C.L.R.O. visited his office but he was out, saw A.F.E.O. stated no doubt sanction of army could be obtained. Ordered FODEN Disinfector to proceed to Divisional baths.	[illegible]
	12.V.18		Visited 156 Brigade Hdquarters, Batt Hq 6 RSF Hdquarters & Regimental aid posts of 4 KOSB + 5 KOSB, these battalions are in the trenches the last on the extreme right of the divisional area + their wounded are evacuated through the 51 Div. Am endeavouring to evacuate them to our own ADS VIMY by relays of bearers.	[illegible]

D. D. & L., London, E.C. (A8004) Wt. W1771/M2031 750,000 5/17 Sch. 52 Forms/C2118/14

Instructions regarding War Diaries and Intelligence Summaries are contained in F. S. Regs., Part II. and the Staff Manual respectively. Title pages will be prepared in manuscript.

WAR DIARY
or
~~INTELLIGENCE~~ SUMMARY.
(Erase heading not required.)

ADMS 52 Div
MAY 1918

Army Form C. 2118.

6

Place	Date	Hour	Summary of Events and Information	Remarks and references to Appendices
CHATEAU D'ACQ	12	V.18	Consulting Surgeon 1st ARMY is coming on 15 to give lecture on various surgical subjects & methods of treatment new to most MO who have only served in EGYPT. The consulting Physician is coming on 15th 16th & 18 to give a series of lectures on gas poisoning a subject on which the MOs of the division have no practical experience. Made arrangements for as many MO as possible to attend.	[illegible]
			Letter from DDMS stating that Dental Surgeons will attend at a Field Ambulance of this Division on Sunday (2) Monday (2) & Wednesday (1) instead of 2 on Wednesday as formerly.	
			Advised DHQ that deep latrine trenches with fly proof seat should be used in the trenches, rather than pails.	
	13	V.18	Interview OC Light railway LIVY with regard to evacuation of patients walking wounded to SAVY	[illegible]
			Examined ground on ARRAS LENS road with a view to a	

D. D. & L., London, E.C. (A8001) Wt. W1771/M2031 750,000 5/17 Sch. 52 Forms/C2118/14

Instructions regarding War Diaries and Intelligence Summaries are contained in F. S. Regs., Part II. and the Staff Manual respectively. Title pages will be prepared in manuscript.

WAR DIARY
or
~~INTELLIGENCE SUMMARY.~~
(Erase heading not required.)

Army Form C. 2118.

ADMS 52 Div
May 1918

7

Place	Date	Hour	Summary of Events and Information	Remarks and references to Appendices
			more advanced Walking wounded Collecting post than the present one but was unable to get a suitable site. The present site is ADS of 3 Lowland Fld at A 8 c 3.3. Visited 1/5th R. S. Reg, the Pioneer batt of this Division. The batt was with 10 Division on the STRUMA front in 1916-1917 & then went to Egypt about August 1917 joining this Division in April 1918 on embarking for France. This batt has had several cases of Malaria. Letter from assistant advisor in pathology 1st ARMY regarding possible malaria carriers in this Division. He wishes to examine 100 cases of men who have suffered from malaria. A list of names of men who have had malignant Malaria has been collected & sent to DMS 1st Army & I have now asked for a return of 100 men who	

D. D. & L., London, E.C. (A8001) Wt. W1 71/M2031 750,000 5/17 Sch. 52 Forms/C2118/14

Instructions regarding War Diaries and Intelligence Summaries are contained in F. S. Regs., Part II. and the Staff Manual respectively. Title pages will be prepared in manuscript.

WAR DIARY
or
INTELLIGENCE SUMMARY.
(Erase heading not required.)

ADMS 52 Div

Army Form C. 2118.

8

Place	Date	Hour	Summary of Events and Information	Remarks and references to Appendices
CHATEAU D'ACQ	13.V.18		have suffered from Malaria.	
			Interviewed D.D.M.S XVIII with reference to various points on evacuation of wounded in the event of active operations	[initials] Arrangements in event of Active Operations APPENDIX 3.
			Report that the M.G. Battalion were still without their Medical panniers which had been indented for but were not available at Adv. Dep. Med Stores.	
	14.V.18		Visited ADS of 3 Lowland FA + Main Dressing Station of 2 Lowland	[initials]
	15.V.18		Inspected men sent from battalions as unfit for duty, with a view of sending them to their base depots to appear before standing medical board.	[initials]
			Consulting Surgeon 1st Army gave demonstration on application of THOMAS splint + various points in Surgery	
			Consulting Physician gave lecture on gassed cases.	

D. D. & L., London, E.C.
(A8001) Wt. W1-71/M2031 750,000 5/17 Sch. 52 Forms/C2118/14

Army Form C. 2118.

WAR DIARY
or
~~INTELLIGENCE SUMMARY.~~
(Erase heading not required.)

Instructions regarding War Diaries and Intelligence Summaries are contained in F. S. Regs., Part II. and the Staff Manual respectively. Title pages will be prepared in manuscript.

A.D.M.S. 52 Div
MAY 1918

9

Place	Date	Hour	Summary of Events and Information	Remarks and references to Appendices
CHATEAU D'ACQ	16.V.18		Lecture on gas. Visited ADS of 2 Lowland at VIMY. In accordance with D.D.M.S. instructions sent 4 TALBOT cars & 2 FORD cars received this month from 112 FA of 16 Div to 77 AMERICAN Division. Reported to 52 Division copy to D.D.M.S. re health of 5 Royal Irish Reg the Pioneer Batt of the Division	Relief of 156 Bde APPENDIX No 2
	18.V.18		Lectures to ... on gas & application of Thomas splints etc finished, visited ADS of 3 Lowland & MDS of 2 Lowland with a view to improving arrangements for treating gas cases	
	19.V.18		Visited units in ST ELOI of the 155 Brigade, water carts not kept in as good condition as they should be. Wrote to Division as to chlorination of water, as there appears to be an impression that the Sanitary Section	

D. D. & L., London, E.C. (A8001) Wt. W1 71/M2031 750,000 5/17 Sch. 52 Forms/C2118/14

Instructions regarding War Diaries and Intelligence Summaries are contained in F. S. Regs., Part II. and the Staff Manual respectively. Title pages will be prepared in manuscript.

WAR DIARY
or
INTELLIGENCE SUMMARY.
(Erase heading not required.)

ADMS 52 Div
MAY 1918

Army Form C. 2118.

10

Place	Date	Hour	Summary of Events and Information	Remarks and references to Appendices
CHATEAU D'ACQ	18.V.18		Chlorinates water in bottles, the Sanitary Section inform me that they chlorinate no water.. Circular memo to MO in water cars	[initials]
	20 V.18		D.MS 1st Army visited MDS of 2 Lowland and ADS of 3 Lowland & ADS of 2 Lowland Fld Ambulance at VIMY. He also visited 6 Royal Irish Regiment with regard to the amount of MALARIA in the battalion which was reported to the Division on 16th.	[initials]
			Visited the ADS of 1 Lowland used as Divisional Rest station and inquired as to the numbers of scabies cases. Large numbers are sent in as scabies many of whom are only suffering from pediculosis. OC F Ambulances instructed to verify the diagnosis where necessary.	
	21.V.18		Conference with DDMS XVIII Corps	[initials]
			D.MS 1st Army having expressed himself as dissatisfied	

D. D. & L., London, E.C. (A8001) Wt. W1 71/M2031 750,000 5/17 Sch. 52 Forms/C2118/14

Army Form C. 2118.

Instructions regarding War Diaries and Intelligence Summaries are contained in F. S. Regs., Part II. and the Staff Manual respectively. Title pages will be prepared in manuscript.

WAR DIARY
or
INTELLIGENCE SUMMARY.
(Erase heading not required.)

Place	Date	Hour	Summary of Events and Information	Remarks and references to Appendices
CHATEAU D'ACQ	21 V 18		with the MDS of [illegible] Fld on account of [illegible] of accommodation & site, it being in a cul de sac as far as evacuations are concerned & being at a cross road where its approach will probably be heavily shelled. With DDMS XVIII Corps chose a site for a new MDS & wrote to Division stating requirements.	[illegible]
	22 V.18		Visited A.D.S. VIMY & RAP. & Relay post. Wrote to DHQ as to necessity of greater care in the trenches as to keeping latrines covered. Many latrines have no covers & those that have are often open owing to men neglecting to shut down the lid.	[illegible]
	23 V 18		Inspected an aid post of the THELUS – NEUVILLE ST VAAST Road with a view to its being strengthened by the R.E. Inspected a cave near it on the LENS ARRAS Road with a view to using	[illegible]

D. D. & L., London, E.C. (A5004) Wt. W1-71/M2031 750,000 5/17 Sch. 52 Forms/C2118/14

Instructions regarding War Diaries and Intelligence Summaries are contained in F. S. Regs., Part II. and the Staff Manual respectively. Title pages will be prepared in manuscript.

WAR DIARY
or
INTELLIGENCE SUMMARY.
(Erase heading not required.)

Army Form C. 2118.

A.D.M.S 52 Div
May 1918

12

Place	Date	Hour	Summary of Events and Information	Remarks and references to Appendices
			as an aid post, it is at present occupied by artillery	
CHATEAU D'ACQ	24.V.18		Conference of D.D.M.S + OC CCSs at PERNES with D.M.S. Present as representing D.D.M.S XVIII Corps. Subject of Conference Coordination of work of Field Ambulances + Casualty Clearing Stations.	
	25.V.18		Visited 2 Lowland Field Ambulance. Found the OC Lt Col DUNNING DSO in bed + was informed that he had been admitted to hospital.	
	26.V.18		Last night the 1/2 Lowland Fld Ambulance + the 1/3 Lowland Field changed over duties, the 1/3 taking over the ADS in the front line + the Main Dressing Station at AUX RIETZ + the 2 Lowland the MDS at ST ELOI + the ADS at AUX RIET for sick + walking wounded	APPENDIX 4.
	27.V.18		At 4.30 am this morning a shell came into a hut of the 1/2 Lowland Fld Ambulance at ST ELOI occupied by the personnel of the unit	

D. D. & L., London, E.C.
(A8001) Wt. W1 71/M2031 750,000 5/17 Sch. 52 Forms/C2118/14

Instructions regarding War Diaries and Intelligence Summaries are contained in F. S. Regs., Part II. and the Staff Manual respectively. Title pages will be prepared in manuscript.

WAR DIARY
or
INTELLIGENCE SUMMARY.
(Erase heading not required.)

ADMS 52 Div
May 1918

Army Form C. 2118.

13

Place	Date	Hour	Summary of Events and Information	Remarks and references to Appendices
CHATEAU D'ACQ	27.V	18	& ~~[illegible]~~ killed 10 OR & wounded 16.	
			Inspected units of the 157 Inf Brigade at ST ELOI	SD
			Gas cases 45 admitted the result of gas shells fired into the area occupied by the 155 Brigade yesterday. None of the cases were severe, all cases appeared to be the result of Yellow Cross Gas	
	28.V.18		With a view to finding a safer Dressing Station than the present one in VIMY visited neighbourhood of MERSEY ALLEY (MAROEUIL MAP) B2 d & with RE officer chose a dugout. Also visited VIMY ADS. The advantages of VIMY ADS is that it is on a road where ambulance cars can run, the disadvantages are that the accommodation is limited, & unsafe as the only accommodation is in cellars half above ground & they cannot be improved without digging for which labour is not at present available	CW
	29.V.18		Held board on men for reclassification at ~~[illegible]~~ ST ELOI	

D. D. & L., London, E.C.
(A8001) Wt. W1 71/M2031 750,000 5/17 Sch. 52 Forms/C2.118/14

Instructions regarding War Diaries and Intelligence Summaries are contained in F. S. Regs., Part II. and the Staff Manual respectively. Title pages will be prepared in manuscript.

WAR DIARY
or
INTELLIGENCE SUMMARY.
(Erase heading not required.)

Army Form C. 2118.

ADMS 52 Div
MAY 1918

14

Place	Date	Hour	Summary of Events and Information	Remarks and references to Appendices
CHATEAU D'ACQ	29 V 18		With Corps Light Railway Officer inspected railway line at F9C at Unsford site of MDS with a view to a siding being put in	
	30 V 18		Visited gas centre of 20 Division by kindness of ADMS 20 Div. Held inspection of men brought up for reclassification at AUX RIETZ	
	31 V 18		Visited Divisional Baths at NEUVILLE ST VAAST with a view of using it as a gas centre. Issued instructions as to using the baths as a gas centre	

[illegible] Col
ADMS 52 Div

D. D. & L., London, E.C.
(A8001) Wt. W1 71/M2031 750,000 5/17 Sch. 52 Forms/C2118/14

ADMS. 52 Divn No. SR/9

Appendix Diary
No. 1.

Copy No 4

Secret

Ramb Operation Order No 1
by
Col. A. J. Macdougall. AMS
ADMS. 52nd Division.

4th May, 1918.

(1) Information. 52nd Division will move from AIRE on 6th 7th and 8th inst. and take over the MERICOURT SECTOR of the Line from the 4th CANADIAN DIVISION.

(2). Personnel will proceed in tactical trains, details to be notified later. Transport and mounted personnel, + horses will move by road under O.C. TRAIN in accordance with attached March Table.

(3). 157 Inf. Bde. Group (including personnel 2nd Low. FLD. AMBCE) will move by tactical Train on 6th instant. to NEUVILLE-ST. VAAST CAMP

(4) 157 Inf. Bde. will relief 11th CANADIAN Bde. of 4th CANADIAN DIVN. in line from T.23.c 50 to northern Boundary of 4th Canadian Division at T.3.B.60 on night 7/8th inst.

(5) 155th Inf Bde (including personnel 3rd Low. Fld. Amb) will be in reserve in ST. ELOY. arriving by tactical Train on 7th instant.

(6). 156th Inf. Bde. (including personnel 1st Low. Fld. Amb.) will be in support in NEUVILLE-ST VAAST arriving by tactical Train on 8th inst.

(7.) Divisional Headquarters will close at AIRE at 1700 on 6th and re-open at CHATEAU ACQ (3/4 mile S.W. of VILLERS AUBOIS).

(8) G.O.C. Inf. Bde. Groups will detail order of entrainment of their units and arrival at entrainment station.

On arrival at detraining station units will be met by guides from Billeting Parties and led to Billeting Areas.

(9). As much Kit as possible will be sent by wagons on the day preceding entrainment. Minimum Officers Kits, second blanket and a proportion of Cooking Utensils can be taken in the tactical Train. Lorries to take these and one day's extra rations for personnel to entraining station will be provided as below (see para 11).

(10) (a) RAILHEAD up to May 6th inclusive AIRE.
from May 7th inclusive ST ELOI.

(b). Transport moving by road 5th 6th and 7th inst. will take two days rations for men and animals with them.

(c). Personnel entraining will do so with rations for the day following entrainment in addition to current day's rations.

(d) All detached parties proceeding by Lorry etc will take three day's rations with them.

(e) Rations for 156th Inf Bde. Group will be drawn on 7th instant from R.S.O. AIRE.

(11)

(11) Lorries, (referred to in para 10)

6th inst - 2 Lorries at H.Q. 157 Inf. Bde. at 6 a.m.
7th inst - 2 " " H.Q 155 " " " 6 a.m.
8th inst - 2 " " H.Q 156 " " " 6 a.m.

(12) Billeting Parties. Orders already issued.

(13). O.C. AMBCES will detail a portion of their motor Ambulance Cars to attend at the entraining station till their Bde. Group has entrained, the remainder being sent forward in time for them to be at the detraining station on the arrival of the first train of their Bde Group.
The cars doing duty at the entraining Station will on completion of entraining of Bde Group rejoin their Ambulances in the Billeting area.

(14). AREA STORES All Area stores which may have been drawn in present Area should be handed into SUB AREA Commandants who will give receipts for them.

(15) STATES. A movement order shewing the number of personnel proceeding by each train will be handed by units to the R.T.O., on arrival at the entraining stations.

[signature]

Colonel AMS.
4 5/18. ADMS. 52nd (Lowland) Division

Copy no 1 to 1st L. Fa.
2 " 2nd L. Fa.
3. " 3rd L. Fa.
4.5 War Diary. ✓
6. File.

Transport and Mounted Personnel March Table.

Date.	Formation.	From	To.	Route.	Under Orders	Remarks.
May 5th	157 Inf. Bde. Group (2nd Low. Fld. Amb.)	AIRE Area.	DIVION.	No restrictions. Suggested – ST HILAIRE FERFAY	OC Train	Billets from Town Major DIVION.
5th	Divisional Headquarters	-do-	-do-	-do-	-do-	-do-
6th	157th Inf. Bde: Group	DIVION.	NEUVILLE ST VAAST	No restrictions Suggested HOUDAIN ESTREECAUCHIE	-do-	Camp and rejoin formation
6th	Divisional Headquarters	-do-	-do-	-do-	-do-	-do-
6th	155th Inf. Bde. Group. (3rd Low. Fld. Amb)	AIRE Area	DIVION	No restrictions Suggested ST. HILAIRE FERFAY	-do-	Billets from Town Major DIVION.
7th	-do-	DIVION.	MONT ST ELOI	No restrictions Suggested – HOUDAIN ESTREECAUCHIE.	-do-	Camp and rejoin formation
7th	156th Inf. Bde. Group (1st Low. Fld. Amb)	AIRE Area	DIVION.	No restrictions Suggested ST HILAIRE FERFAY	-do-	Billets from Town Major DIVION.
8th	-do-	DIVION.	NEUVILLIE ST. VAAST	No restrictions Suggested: HOUDAIN ESTREECAUCHIE	-do-	Camp and rejoin formation

NOTE:- No traffic to proceed through BRUAY.

Secret.　　S.R. 15　　Copy No 5

R.A.M.C. Operation Order. No 2.
By.
Colonel A. J. MacDougall. AMS.
ADMS. 52nd. Division = 5th May. 1918.

(1). On arrival at de-training Station O.C. 2nd Lowland Field Ambce. will report to ADMS. 4th Canadian Division. at AUX RIETZ to take over Dressing Stations etc. from 12th Canadian Field Ambulance.

(2). The following will be taken over:- Main Dressing Station at AUX RIETZ, Advanced Dressing Station at LA. CHAUDIERE, and VIMY VILLAGE. Relay Post at KURTON, BRUNSWICK ROAD, T. 21. c. 7. 6. & EMBANKMENT. (not shewn on map). T. 13. B. 5.5. and DARTMOUTH. T. 8. A. 78. Regimental Aid Posts at HAYTER, TEDDIE, RAILWAY EMBANKMENT, T. 26 a. c. 9. PEGGIE (Reference BLUE MAP in Medical Arrangements, 4th Canadian Division, sent under my S.R. 11 dated today, 5/5/18).
Relief will be completed on 7/5/18..

(3). The 12th Canadian Field Ambulance. relieved by the 2nd Lowland Field Am will hand over Blankets, Stretchers, Thomas Splints, and number taken over will be reported to this office.

(4). Equipment sent up to A.D.S. will be by means of Ambulance. Motor Cars, and not by Horse Transport. Personnel going up by day will proceed by parties not exceeding 10 (ten) in each party.

(5). Advanced Party of Officers and other ranks, numbers to be decided in consultation with O.C. 12th Canadian Field Ambulance, will go to the A.D.S and Relay Posts, and R.A.P. on 6/5/18 in order to become familiar with the Posts and locality and should be able to point out R.A.P. to M.O. of the 157 Brigade. on the Brigade coming into the line.

(6) One Squad of 4 Bearers will be located in each R.A.P. and Relay Post.

Evacuations.
(7). For the present cases will be evacuated from A.D.S. by Motor Ambulance. Notification will be sent later re evacuation by trams.
Evacuations from M.D.S. at AUX RIETZ will be carried out by 8th M.A.C. stationed there to the group of C.C.S. stationed at AUBIGNEY.

(8) A Report to this Office will be rendered shewing distribution of personnel at R.A.Ps., Relay Posts, etc.,

(9). Report completion of move to this Office.

(10). acknowledge.

Copy No1. to 2nd L.F.A.
" " 2. " ADMS. 4th. Canadian DIVISION.
" " 3. " War Diary.
" " 4. " " " ✓
" " 5 " FILE.
Issued 11.15 pm.

[signature]
Colonel A.M.
A.D.M.S. 52nd Divisio

Appendix No. 2.

SECRET.

Reference [illegible] ORDER No. 1[illegible].

I. INTENTION. 1[illegible]th Inf. Bde. will relieve the 1[illegible]th Inf. Bde. in the Right Section of the Divisional Line on night of 13th/14th inst., and on relief the 1[illegible]th Inf. Bde. will take over the billets and dispositions of the 1[illegible]th Inf. Bde.

II. DETAIL.

1st Lowland Field Ambulance.

Headquarters:	[illegible] AU BOIS:	X.1[illegible].c.9.9.
Transport:	-do-	-do-
[illegible]	-do-	-do-

2nd Lowland Field Ambulance.

Headquarters.	[illegible]	A.[illegible].c.[illegible].
Transport:	[illegible]	
M. D. S.	[illegible]	A.[illegible].c.[illegible].
A. D. S.	[illegible]	[illegible].a.0.d.
	La [illegible]	[illegible].1[illegible].c.[illegible].
Relay Posts.	[illegible].1[illegible].b.7.[illegible]., [illegible].b.[illegible].7., [illegible].a.[illegible].9.	
R. A. P.	[illegible].c.[illegible]., [illegible].1[illegible].c.[illegible]., [illegible].a.c.1. [illegible].a.[illegible]., [illegible].1[illegible].a.0.[illegible].	

3rd Lowland Field Ambulance.

Headquarters:	St. ELOY.	[illegible].c.9.[illegible].
Transport:	-do-	-do-
M. D. S.	-do-	-do-
A. D. S.	-	A.[illegible].c.[illegible].

III. MEDICAL ARRANGEMENTS [illegible] DIVISIONAL LINE.

All cases of sick and wounded of troops in the trenches will be evacuated through the A.D.Ss. of 2nd Lowland Field Ambulance with the exception of those from the R.A.P. of the Right Battalion of the Right Section which are evacuated through the 51st Division to Collecting Post, [illegible].1[illegible].c.[illegible].1.

Sick of Units in neighbourhood of Neuville St. VAAST to A.D.S. of 3rd Lowland Field Ambulance.

Sick of Units in neighbourhood of St. ELOY to M.D.S. of 3rd Lowland Field Ambulance.

IV. ACKNOWLEDGE.

Colonel, A.M.S.,

13th May, 1918. A.D.M.S., 52nd (Lowland) Division.

Copy No. 1 to	"A" Branch.	Copy No. 7 to	1st L.F.A.	
2	"Q" Branch.	8	2nd L.F.A.	
3	15[illegible] Inf.Bde.	9	3rd L.F.A.	
4	15[illegible] Inf.Bde.	10 ✓	Diary.	
~~[illegible]~~	~~[illegible]~~.	11 ✓	Diary.	
5	52nd Bn.M.G.C.	12	File.	
6	52nd D.I.[illegible].(P)			

War Diary

APPENDIX No 3.

AMMENDMENTS TO "MEDICAL ARRANGEMENTS IN THE EVENT OF ACTIVE OPERATIONS - 52nd (LOWLAND) DIVISION." (17/5/18.)

****

For "2nd Low. Fld. Amb" read "3rd Low. Fld. Amb." throughout.
For "3rd Low. Fld. Amb." read "2nd Low. Fld. Amb." throughout.

H.Q., 52nd Divn.
26th MAY, 1918.

Colonel, A. M. S.,
A.D.M.S., 52nd (Lowland) Division.

(Copies to all recipients of above arrangements)

Diary

SECRET. Copy No. 11

MEDICAL ARRANGEMENTS No. 2
52nd (Lowland) DIVISION,

Reference:- Army Map "B", 1/40,000. 17th May, 1918.

1. LOCATIONS.
A.D.M.S. Office:- CHATEAU ACQ. - W.30.b.4.5.
1st Lowland Fld. Amb:- Divisional Rest Station, VILLERS AU BOIS - X.19.c.9.9.

2nd Lowland Fld. Amb:- Main Dressing Station - AUX RIETZ - A.8.c.5.5.
Advanced Dressing Stations- VIMY - T.25.a.9.4. and LA CHAUDERIE - S.18.c.9.3.

Regimental Aid Posts.	Relay Posts.
T.8.c.9.5.	T.13.b.7.8.
T.16.a.6.9.	T.20.b.2.7.
T.28.a.4.1.	T.28.a.3.9.
B.2.a.9.8.	A.11.b.3.9.
B.15.a.0.8.	

3rd Lowland Fld. Amb:- Main Dressing Station - ST ELOY - F.8.c.9.4.
Advanced Dressing Station - A.8.c.8.8.

2. WOUNDED. Normally, all wounded will pass through the A.D.S., 2nd Lowland Fld. Amb., whence they will be evacuated by Ambulance Motor Cars of the Field Ambulance to the M.D.S. from which they will be evacuated by M.A.C.
Wounded collected in R.A.P., B.15.a.0.8. will be evacuated ~~from~~ through the 51st Division A.D.S.

3. SICK. Sick of Units in the trenches will be evacuated through A.D.S. to M.D.S. of 2nd Low. Fld. Amb. and thence transferred to A.D.S. of 3rd Low. Fld. Amb.
Sick of Units in neighbourhood of NEUVILLE ST VAAST will be admitted to A.D.S. of 3rd Low. Fld. Amb. and sent to M.D.S. of 3rd Low. Fld. Amb. at ST ELOY where they are either evacuated by M.A.C. or transferred to Divisional Rest Station of 1st Low. Fld. Amb.
Sick of Units in neighbourhood of ST ELOY will be admitted to 3rd Low. Fld. Amb.

4. WALKING WOUNDED. During heavy fighting, when there are numbers of walking wounded, the A.D.S. of the 3rd Low. Fld. Amb. will be used as a Walking Wounded Collecting Centre and will be evacuated by Light Railway or Motor Lorry, or other means as directed.

5. GASSED CASES. Severe cases will be evacuated to C.C.S. from the M.D.S., 2nd Low. Fld. Amb. in the usual manner by M.A.C.
Slight and doubtful cases will be transferred from 2nd Low. Fld. Amb. to 1st Low. Fld. Amb.

[signature]
Colonel, A. M. S.,
A. D. M. S., 52nd (Lowland) DIVISION.

Copies No. 1 to 4 to "G"
5 " "A"
6 "
7 " 1st L.F.A.
8 " 2nd L.F.A.
9 " 3rd L.F.A.
10 " D.D.M.S., XVIII Corps.
11 " A.D.M.S., 20th Divn.
12 " Diary.
13 " Diary File

OR 60

Diary

SECRET. COPY No. 11

MEDICAL ARRANGEMENTS IN THE EVENT OF ACTIVE OPERATIONS

52nd (LOWLAND) DIVISION.

17th MAY, 1918.

1. EVACUATION.

(a) In the event of active operations, stretcher and sitting cases will be evacuated through the A.D.S. to M.D.S. of the 2nd Low. Fld. Ambulance; walking cases to A.D.S. of 3rd Low.Fld.Amb.(Walking Wounded Collecting Post.) Cases will be evacuated by hand carry, wheeled stretchers, ambulance cars and wagons, tram trollies and light railway according to circumstances. O.C., 2nd Low. Fld. Amb. is responsible for making arrangements for trains between A.D.S. and M.D.S.

(b) Stretcher and sitting cases will be evacuated from M.D.S. of 2nd Low. Fld. Amb. to C.C.S. by means of M.A.C. cars.

(c) Walking wounded will be evacuated from A.D.S. of 3rd Low. Fld. Amb. to detraining centre at V.29.a.75.65., near MINGOVAL, by means of light railway.

O.C., 3rd Low. Fld. Amb. is responsible for making arrangements for trains on the light railway between his A.D.S. and detraining station. All applications for trains will be made to "Traffic Control" XIVY. An N.C.O. and Orderly will accompany each train. A detraining party of 1st Low. Fld. Amb. is already at the detraining station and four motor lorries will be attached for removing patients from the detraining station to the C.C.S.

NO stretcher cases will be evacuated by this train.

One motor lorry and one motor ambulance car will be on duty at the Walking Wounded Collecting Post; the former for evacuation of walking wounded to C.C.S., the latter for cases which may need stretchers.

(d) SICK.- Serious cases will be sent to M.D.S., 2nd Low. Fld. Amb.and thence on to C.C.S. by M.A.C. cars. Slight cases will be sent to M.D.S., 2nd Low. Fld. Amb.and thence on to Divisional Rest Station by means of Horsed Ambulances of 1st Low. Fld. Amb.

2. PERSONNEL.

O.C., 3rd Low. Fld. Amb. will reinforce the 2nd Low. Fld. Amb. with his bearers to work under the orders of O.C., 2nd Low. Fld. Amb. who will supply guides and allot the ground that each Section will work over.

O.C., 3rd Low. Fld. Amb. will detail two officers to assist at the Main Dressing Stn of the 2nd Low. Fld. Amb.

M.O.i/c, Divisional R.S. will also be available for duty at the M.D.S. of 2nd Low. Fld. Amb.

O.C., 3rd Low. Fld. Amb.will arrange for feeding of walking wounded at his A.D.S.

O.C., 1st Low. Fld. Amb. will hold his bearer sub-divisions in reserve, ready to reinforce as necessary.

3. TRANSPORT.

AMBULANCE CARS.- Divisional Ambulance Cars will be used for evacuating in the Divisional Area and will not proceed to C.C.S. without orders from this office.

Ten M.A.C. cars (which are under the orders of the O.C.,M.A.C.) will evacuate from M.D.S., AUX RIETZ to C.C.S.

O.C., 3rd Low. Fld. Amb. will place his Ambulance Cars, less two, at the disposal of the O.C., 2nd Low. Fld. Amb.for use in evacuating from A.D.S., 2nd Low. Fld. Amb.

O.C., 1st Low. Fld. Amb. will hold his cars in reserve.

Two horsed Ambulance Wagons of 1st Low. Fld. Amb. will be placed at the disposal of O.C., 2nd Low. Fld. Amb. for evacuating cases to the Divisional Rest Station.

3. Transport (contd)

Car Relay Posts between the A.D.S. and M.D.S. of 2nd Low. Fld. Amb. will be arranged by O.C., 2nd Low. Fld. Amb.

4. MEDICAL.

ANTI-TETANIC Serum will be given at M.D.Ss, except, (a) walking wounded admitted to A.D.S., 3rd Low. Fld. Amb. (Walking Wounded Collecting Post) where it will be given if not already done so, (b) other cases evacuated direct to a C.C.S. from an A.D.S.

Medical Comforts - Field Ambulances will indent direct on S.S.O. for food and medical comforts for patients.

5. GENERAL.

All changes in A.D.Ss, Relay Posts, W.A.Ps will be reported to this office at once.

Applications for bearers, cars etc. will be made to this office.

Colonel, A. M. S.,

A. D. M. S., 52nd (LOWLAND) DIVISION.

Copies No. 1 to 4 to "G"
5 " "A"
6 " 1st L.F.A.
7 " 2nd L.F.A.
8 " 3rd L.F.A.
9 " D.D.M.S., XVIII Corps.
10 " A.D.M.S., 20th Divn.
11 " Diary.
12 " Diary.
13 " File.

APPENDIX No 4

SR.72

S E C R E T.

Copy No. 7

M.A.M.S. OPERATION ORDER No. 3
BY
A.D.M.S., 52nd (LOWLAND) DIVISION.

23rd May,1918.

1. MOVE. The 2nd Low. Fld. Amb. will be relieved by the 3rd Low. Fld. Amb. on the night of [illegible] instant and the existing M.D.S., A.D.Ss and Relay Posts of the 2nd Low. Fld. Amb. occupied by the 3rd Low. Fld. Amb. The 2nd Low. Fld.Amb. on relief will take over and occupy the M.D.S. and A.D.S. vacated
2. by 3rd Low. Fld. Amb.

2. TRANSPORT. The Transport of the 2nd Low. Fld. Amb. at VILLERS AU BOIS will be used to assist in the move of that Unit and will be parked thereafter in the vicinity of the M.D.S. in ST ELOY.
Transport and heavy stores of 3rd Low. Fld. Amb. not actually required in the evacuating zone will be parked at VILLERS AU BOIS on site vacated by Transport of 2nd Low. Fld. Amb. previously there.

3. DETAILS. O.C., 2nd Low. Fld. Amb. will furnish in writing to O.C., 3rd Low. Fld. Amb. the information as to position, trench stores and strength of personnel at the various posts.

4. EVACUATION. On relief being completed, Medical Arrangements No. 2, Medical Arrangements in the event of Active Operations (17/5/18) and Arrangements in the Event of Severe Gas Attack (20/5/18) will remain as at present, reading 2nd Low. Fld. Amb. for 3rd Low. Fld. Amb. and 3rd Low. Fld. Amb. for 2nd Low. Fld. Amb.

5. GENERAL. In order to avoid as much as possible unnecessary movement, such stores as wheeled and ordinary stretchers, blankets, Soyers stoves, spare dressings, drugs etc will be taken over by the relieving Unit.
The 118 stretchers taken over ~~xx xxx~~ from the Canadian Fld. Amb. will be handed over to O.C.,3rd Low. Fld. Amb.
As many other stores as possible will not be moved ~~xxxxxx xxxx~~ but changed like for like.
Special clothing and apparatus for use in case of gas attacks will be kept in their present locations and handed over.

6. RELIEFS. Reliefs will be notified to this office.

7. ACKNOWLEDGE.

A.J. MacDougall

Colonel, A. M. S.,
A. D. M. S., 52nd (Lowland) DIVISION.

Copy No. 1.to 2nd L.F.A.
2. 3rd L.F.A.
3. 1st L.F.A.
4. D.D.M.S.,XVIII Corps.
5. H.Q., 52nd Divn.
6.
7.) Diary. ✓
8. File.

War Diary

S E C R E T. Copy No. 11
****

MEDICAL ARRANGEMENTS No. 3
52nd (LOWLAND) DIVISION.
****

Reference Army Map "D", 1/40,000. 26th MAY, 1918.

1. LOCATIONS.

A.D.M.S. Office:- CHATEAU ACQ. - W.30.b.4.5.
1st Low. Fld. Amb.- Divisional Rest Station,
VILLERS AU BOIS - X.19.c.9.9.
2nd Low. Fld. Amb.- M. D. S. - ST ELOY - F.8.c.9.4.
A. D. S. - A.8.c.8.8.
3rd Low. Fld. Amb.- M. D. S. - AUX RIETZ.- A.8.c.5.5.
A. D. S. - VIMY - T.25.a.9.4.
A. D. S. - LA CHAUDERIE - S.18.c.9.3.

Regimental Aid Posts.	Relay Posts.
T.8.c.9.5.	T.13.b.7.8.
T.13.c.3.9.	T.20.b.2.7.
T.22.a.4.1.	T.2?.d.8.9.
B.2.a.9.8.	A.11.b.3.9.
B.13.a.0.8.	

2. WOUNDED. Normally, all wounded will pass through the A.D.S., 3rd Low. Fld. Amb., whence they will be evacuated by Ambulance Motor Cars of the Field Ambulance to the M.D.S. from which they will be evacuated by M. A. C.

Wounded collected in R. A. P., B.13.a.0.8. will be evacuated through the 51st Division A. D. S.

3. SICK. Sick of Units in the trenches will be evacuated through A. D. S. to M. D. S. of 3rd Low. Fld. Amb. and thence transferred to A. D. S. of 2nd Low. Fld. Amb.

Sick of Units in neighbourhood of NEUVILLE ST VAAST ~~[illegible]~~ will be admitted to A. D. S. of 2nd Low. Fld. Amb. and sent to M. D. S. of 2nd Low. Fld. Amb. at ST ELOY where they are either evacuated by M.A.C. or transferred to Divisional Rest Station of 1st Low. Fld. Amb.

Sick of Units in neighbourhood of ST ELOY will be admitted to 2nd Low. Fld. Amb.

4. WALKING WOUNDED. During heavy fighting, when there are numbers of walking wounded, the A. D. S. of the 2nd Low. Fld. Amb. will be used as a Walking Wounded Collecting Centre and will be evacuated by Light Railway or Motor Lorry, or other means as directed.

5. GASSED CASES. Severe cases will be evacuated to C. C. S. from the M. D. S., 3rd Low. Fld. Amb. in the usual manner by M. A. C.

Slight and doubtful cases will be transferred from 3rd Low. Fld. Amb. to 1st Low. Fld. Amb.

6. ACKNOWLEDGE.

A J MacDonald
Colonel, A. M. S.,
A. D. M. S., 52nd (LOWLAND) DIVISION.

Copies No.1 to 4 to "G"
5 " "A"
6 " 1st L.F.A.
7 " 2nd L.F.A.
8 " 3rd L.F.A.
9 " D.D.M.S.

Copy No.10 to A.D.M.S., 20thDiv.
11 " Diary.
12 " Diary.
13 " File.

Confidential

War Diary

of

A.D.M.S. 52nd Division

FROM 1ST TO 30TH JUNE, 1918.

(VOLUME 6)

17 June 1918

Vol 3

Instructions regarding War Diaries and Intelligence Summaries are contained in F. S. Regs., Part II. and the Staff Manual respectively. Title pages will be prepared in manuscript.

WAR DIARY
or
~~INTELLIGENCE~~ SUMMARY.
(Erase heading not required.)

ADMS 52 Dn

JUNE - 1918

Army Form C. 2118.

1

Place	Date	Hour	Summary of Events and Information	Remarks and references to Appendices
CHATEAU D'ACQ	1 VI 18		Visited 155 Brigade in the line with Div Gas officer as it was reported there had been heavy gas shelling last night & early this morning. No evidence was obtained that there was any gas except Blue Cross & the bold gas cases were 6, the result of a previous shelling of VIMY village with yellow cross shells two days previous. Wrote to G S about improving ADS at VIMY With Corps Light railway officer visited proposed site of MDS at F 9 c, work of erecting huts has been commenced	
	2 VI 18		Visited 2 Lowland Fld Ambulance & pointed out to O C necessity for many improvements. The 156 Brigade was relieved by 157 Infant Brigade in the Right Section & on relief went into reserve at ST ELOI	

D. D. & L., London, E.C. (A8031) Wt. W1 71/M2031 750,000 5/17 Sch. 52 Forms/C2118/14

Instructions regarding War Diaries and Intelligence Summaries are contained in F. S. Regs., Part II. and the Staff Manual respectively. Title pages will be prepared in manuscript.

WAR DIARY
or
INTELLIGENCE SUMMARY.
(Erase heading not required.)

Army Form C. 2118.

ADMS 52 Div
JUNE 1918
2

Place	Date	Hour	Summary of Events and Information	Remarks and references to Appendices
CHATEAU D'ACQ	4. VI. 18		Inspected units of 156 Brigade at St ELOI. Report to Q that there was overcrowding of the huts & recommended either the erection of additional huts or the bivouacing of men. There has been an increase of PUO recently, this does not suggest MALARIA or TRENCH FEVER, the symptoms are sudden onset, headache pain in back, in some cases bronchial catarrh, a characteristic of the disease is that several men in a unit are affected at the same time in a platoon or coy, while the rest of the unit is free other coys being affected later.	[initials]
	5 VI. 18		Visited Regimental Aid Post of 157 Infantry Brigade in Right section. Wrote to Division on latrines in the trenches pointing out that the latrines were far from fly proof	[initials]
	6. VI. 18		Visited with DDMS XVIII Corps & AA + QMG 52 Div the 1/1 Lowland Fld ambulance & a new A.D.S in MERSEY ALLEY B2 x 94	[initials]

D. D. & L., London, E.C.
(A8004) Wt. W1 71/M2031 750,000 5/17 Sch. 52 Forms/C2118/14

Army Form C. 2118.

WAR DIARY
or
~~INTELLIGENCE SUMMARY.~~
(Erase heading not required.)

Instructions regarding War Diaries and Intelligence Summaries are contained in F. S. Regs., Part II. and the Staff Manual respectively. Title pages will be prepared in manuscript.

ADMS 52 DIV
JUNE 1918

3

Place	Date	Hour	Summary of Events and Information	Remarks and references to Appendices
CHATEAU D'ACQ	6.VI.18		This ADS has been taken into use instead of the one at VIMY as the latter has no shell proof accommodation & it is impossible with labour available to dig a sufficiently large one. The present one is a deep dugout behind a railway embankment with three entrances capable of holding 38 stretcher cases.	
	7.VI.18		Inspected 2 Lowland Fld Ambulance their accommodation is poor & as many shells have fallen close to their site patients have not been kept longer than is possible.	
			Work progressing at new M.D.S at F 9 c central is progressing a loop line has been made & 6 huts erected	
	8.VI.18		A conference of DDMS & ADMS at No 4 Canadian CCS to meet the DMS 1st Army DADMS of this Division attended	
			Visited ADS at B 2 d 9.4 with a view to finding increased accommodation the only method of doing this will be to dig into the side of the embankment of the railway & erect shelters.	

D. D. & L., London, E.C. (A8001) Wt. W1 71/M2031 750,000 5/17 Sch. 52 Forms/C2118/14

Instructions regarding War Diaries and Intelligence Summaries are contained in F. S. Regs., Part II. and the Staff Manual respectively. Title pages will be prepared in manuscript.

WAR DIARY
or
INTELLIGENCE SUMMARY.
(Erase heading not required.)

Army Form C. 2118.

ADMS 52 Div.
JUNE 1918.

4

Place	Date	Hour	Summary of Events and Information	Remarks and references to Appendices
	8.VI.18		The sanitation of the area west of the FARBUS VIMY railway line is very bad, food thrown about, latrines not fly proof & uncared for, reported this to the Division	(A)
	9.VI.18		Attended at DDMS XVIII Corps office at an interview Major Burns in which he wished to see the DDMS regarding an unfavourable report rendered on him by ADMS & GOC 52 Div.	(A)
			Visited a hot air Disinfestor for freeing clothing of lice invented by Capt ORR of the 3 Canadian Sanitary Section.	
	10 VI.18		Four American Medical officers reported for duty	
			Examined road in S30 with a view to an ADS this road is on the ridge above VIMY & at its northern end is in a deep cutting but though protected from the east, is fully exposed to enemy fire from the north & is also not very accessible from the main road.	HW
			There is an increase in the number of PUO cases in the Division, as noted under 4 VI 18	

D. D. & L., London, E.C. (A8001) Wt. W1 71/M2031 750,000 5/17 Sch. 52 Forms/C2118/14

Instructions regarding War Diaries and Intelligence Summaries are contained in F. S. Regs., Part II. and the Staff Manual respectively. Title pages will be prepared in manuscript.

WAR DIARY
or
INTELLIGENCE SUMMARY.
(Erase heading not required.)

Army Form C. 2118.

A.D.M.S. 52 Div

JUNE 1918

5

Place	Date	Hour	Summary of Events and Information	Remarks and references to Appendices
	11 VI 18		Visited MAISNEL BOUCHE with D.D.M.S. XVIII Corps with a view of obtaining accommodation for the 1/2 Lowland F.A. This ambulance is at present stationed at St ELOI, there accommodation for patients is small & scattered, the village is frequently shelled (the ambulance recently lost 12 killed & 16 wounded from 1 shell) & it is not advisable to keep patients there. A good site & accommodation selected & application made to Corps for it. The 156 Inf Brigade relieved the 155 Inf Brigade in the line & in support, the latter coming into reserve in St ELOI	(a)
	12 VI 18		Visited the 9th R.F.A Brigade & Units South of THELLUS. The artillery is scattered & are some considerable distance from the Advanced Dressing Stations. They are in rear of the ADS except in the case of the forward guns which are near the ADS. No of PUO cases evacuated yesterday 50.	(b)

D. D. & L., London, E.C. (A8001) Wt. W1-71/M2031 750,000 5/17 Sch. 52 Forms/C2118/14

Instructions regarding War Diaries and Intelligence Summaries are contained in F. S. Regs., Part II. and the Staff Manual respectively. Title pages will be prepared in manuscript.

WAR DIARY
or
~~INTELLIGENCE~~ SUMMARY.
(Erase heading not required.)

Army Form C. 2118.

ADMS 52 Div
JUNE 1918

6

Place	Date	Hour	Summary of Events and Information	Remarks and references to Appendices
	12 VI 18		2 officers & 4 other ranks RAMC proceeded to 1st ARMY RAMC School	[initials]
	13 VI 18		Visited 155 Inf Brigade in ST ELOI. Reported to DHQ various insanitary conditions in FRASER camp	
			PUO evacuated yesterday 54	[initials]
			Wrote to DDMS pointed out the shortage of Medical officers & asking that reinforcements might be expedited.	
	14 VI 18		Visited 1 Lowland FA 1 Lowland FA at VILLER AUX BOIS + Reinforcement Camp in neighbourhood.	[initials]
			PUO cases evacuated 87.	
	15 VI 18		Visited MDS 3 Lowland FA & machine gun battalion also BATH at NEUVILLE ST VAAST	
			2 Lowland FA moved to ambulance site at LES 4 VENT as it was not possible to obtain the site at MAISNEL BOUCHE	[initials]

D. D. & L., London, E.C. (A8004) Wt. W1771/M2031 750,000 5/17 Sch. 52 Forms/C2118/14

Instructions regarding War Diaries and Intelligence Summaries are contained in F. S. Regs., Part II. and the Staff Manual respectively. Title pages will be prepared in manuscript.

WAR DIARY
or
INTELLIGENCE SUMMARY.
(*Erase heading not required.*)

Army Form C. 2118.

ADMS 52 Div
JUNE 1918

7

Place	Date	Hour	Summary of Events and Information	Remarks and references to Appendices
	15 VI 18		Number of PUO cases evacuated yesterday 35.	[initials]
	16 VI 18		Visited A.D.S & RAP in left section. Number of PUO cases evacuated 105	[initials]
	17 VI 18		Visited 2 Lowland FA at LES 4 VENTS. The 1/4th RSF & 1/4 KOSB are having large numbers of cases of P.U.O. PUO cases admitted 119 evacuated 71	[initials]
	18 VI 18		Visited DDMS XVIII with reference to obtaining more stretchers & blankets to increase accommodation of Field ambulances to deal with cases as evacuations to No 1 CCS have been suspended for the present. Recommended to Division that the huts in ST ELOI camps at present occupied by 155 Brigade should be disinfected before being used by 157 Brigade who come into them on 20th. All RMO instructed to arrange with their units to have a permanganate	[initials]

D. D. & L., London, E.C. (A8001) Wt. W1-71/M2031 750,000 5/17 Sch. 52 Forms/C2118/14

Instructions regarding War Diaries and Intelligence Summaries are contained in F. S. Regs., Part II. and the Staff Manual respectively. Title pages will be prepared in manuscript.

WAR DIARY
or
INTELLIGENCE SUMMARY.

(Erase heading not required.)

Army Form C. 2118.

ADMS 52 Div
JUNE 1918

8

Place	Date	Hour	Summary of Events and Information	Remarks and references to Appendices
	18.VI.18.		of potash mouth wash & gargle issued twice a day to all ranks, strength 1gr to 1 pint	
			Particular attention called to the cleansing of teeth & of ventilation of huts.	(W)
			PUO cases admitted 157 evac 135	
	19.VI.18		Requested 52 Division to publish as Divisional order the following	
			Precautions against PUO.	(W)
			1 All ranks whether sick or not will use morning & evening, as a gargle & mouth wash a permanganate solution which is being issued. This solution must not be swallowed	Appendix 1
			2 Units having Medical officers may obtain the permanganate in crystal form from the nearest Field Ambulance & the Medical Officers will issue the permanganate in solution in the strength already indicated to them.	
			3 Units having no Medical officer may obtain the solution ready made from the nearest Field Ambulance	
			4 Gargling will take place as a parade under an officer.	

D. D. & L., London, E.C.
(A8004) Wt W1771/M2031 750,000 5/17 Sch. 52 Forms/C2118/14

Instructions regarding War Diaries and Intelligence Summaries are contained in F. S. Regs., Part II. and the Staff Manual respectively. Title pages will be prepared in manuscript.

WAR DIARY
or
INTELLIGENCE SUMMARY.
(Erase heading not required.)

Army Form C. 2118.

ADMS 52 Div
JUNE 1918

9

Place	Date	Hour	Summary of Events and Information	Remarks and references to Appendices
	19 VI 18		Held a medical Board by order of DGMS on 302308 Pte GILLIES 1/5 A&SH as to his fitness for service. PUO cases adm 86 evacuated 51	AD
	20 VI 18		155 Inf Brigade relieved 157 Brigade in the line, the latter brigade coming into reserve in ST ELOI, all huts occupied by 155 Brigade disinfected with cresol.	AD
			DDMS informed me that it had been decided to form an auxiliary hospital of 800 as part of 2 Lowland FA to hold PUO cases to be open at CAMBLAIN L'ABBE as soon as possible so as to obviate the necessity of evacuating cases of PUO who will shortly be fit for duty. PUO cases admitted 285 evac 196	
	21 VI 18		Auxiliary Hospital opens at CAMBLAIN L'ABBE with assistance of personnel from various units MO 3 OR 117. This hospital is	AD

D. D. & L., London, E.C.
(A8204) Wt W1771/M2031 750,000 5/17 Sch. 52 Forms/C2118/14

Army Form C. 2118.

WAR DIARY
or
INTELLIGENCE SUMMARY.
(Erase heading not required.)

Instructions regarding War Diaries and Intelligence Summaries are contained in F. S. Regs., Part II. and the Staff Manual respectively. Title pages will be prepared in manuscript.

ADMS 62 Div
June 1918

10

Place	Date	Hour	Summary of Events and Information	Remarks and references to Appendices
			for PUO cases not only from this Division but from the 20th & 24 Division & Corps troops, the cases will be kept in the hospital treated & returned to duty & will not be evacuated to CCS	
			Camps at RISPIN & VILLER AU BOIS are also being taken over for the same purpose	
			PUO cases in Division admitted 156 evacuated 40	
	22.VI.18		Telephonic instruction from the DDMS XVIII that the scheme of using camps at VILLERS & RISPIN as hospitals for keeping PUO has been cancelled & all PUO cases are now to be evacuated to CCS or discharged to duty.	
			PUO cases in Division admitted 41 evacuated 23	
	23.VI.18		Visited VILLERS & LE PENDU camp	
			PUO in Division admitted 36 evacuated 148.	

D. D. & L., London, E.C.
(A8004) Wt W177/M2031 750,000 5/17 Sch. 52 Forms/C2118/14

Army Form C. 2118.

WAR DIARY
or
~~INTELLIGENCE SUMMARY.~~
(Erase heading not required.)

Instructions regarding War Diaries and Intelligence Summaries are contained in F. S. Regs., Part II. and the Staff Manual respectively. Title pages will be prepared in manuscript.

ADMS 52 Div
JUNE 1918

11

Place	Date	Hour	Summary of Events and Information	Remarks and references to Appendices
	24.VI.	18	Capt JOBSON SCOTT T.F. RAMC reported for duty in relief of Lt Col DUNNING evacuated sick to ENGLAND to take over command of 1/2 Lowland FA	
			Inspected units of 157 Inf Brigade in Reserve at ST ELOI this Brigade except the 1/5 A+SH has had very little PUO.	[initials]
			Wrote to AHQ, Q 52 Div pointing out that the various Camps at ST ELOI & NEUVILLE ST WAAST were defective in meat safes & means of protecting food from flies.	
			PUO cases - admitted 28 evacuated 16	
	25.VI.18		Examined GRANGE Subway with a view to using it as a Reserve dressing station, examination disappointing as although the subway extends for about 1200 yds it is almost only a tunnel with little accommodation	[initials]
			Examined CAMPBELL road & track to LA FOLIE farm & road leading from the latter to LENS ARRAS road with a view to finding a	

Instructions regarding War Diaries and Intelligence Summaries are contained in F. S. Regs., Part II. and the Staff Manual respectively. Title pages will be prepared in manuscript.

WAR DIARY
or
~~INTELLIGENCE SUMMARY.~~
(Erase heading not required.)

Army Form C. 2118.

ADMS 52 Div
June 1918

12

Place	Date	Hour	Summary of Events and Information	Remarks and references to Appendices
			a route that will miss the cross roads at the interjunction of the LENS-ARRAS Rd & the THELLUS & NEUVILLE ST WAAST ROAD & also the LA TARGETTE CROSS ROAD. Such a road does not at present exist practicable for motor cars.	W
			Visited FABBUS NORTH A.D.S	
			PUO cases admitted 47 evacuated 38	
	26.VI.18		PUO cases admitted 33 " 36	
			Visited ADS & RAP in Right ~~[illegible]~~ section area	W
	27.VI.18		PUO cases admitted 30 evacuated 30	W
			Visited left Section area	
	29.VI.18		Visited D.R.S & own men for classification	
			PUO cases admitted 30 evacuated 40	W
	30.VI.18		Classification Board.	
			WIRE from DDMS stating that up to 200 cases should be kept in Divisional area & not evacuated to base	W

D. D. & L., London, E.C.
(A8204) Wt W1771/M2031 750,000 5/17 Sch. 52 Forms/C2118/14

Instructions regarding War Diaries and Intelligence Summaries are contained in F. S. Regs., Part II. and the Staff Manual respectively. Title pages will be prepared in manuscript.

WAR DIARY
or
~~INTELLIGENCE SUMMARY.~~

(Erase heading not required.)

Army Form C. 2118.

ADMS 52 Div

JUNE 1918

13

Place	Date	Hour	Summary of Events and Information	Remarks and references to Appendices
	30 VI 18		Auxiliary Hospital CAMBLAIN L'ABBEYE Closed 156 Inf Brigade relieved 157 Inf Brigade yesterday, the latter coming into reserve at ST ELOI	[illegible]

A. J. MacDougall Col
ADMS 52 Div

D. D. & L., London, E.C.
(A8304) Wt W177/M2031 750,000 5/17 Sch. 52 Forms/C2118/14

APPENDIX 1

A.D.M.S., 52nd Divn. No. R.948/H.

ALL UNITS.

---

1 The present epidemic of P.O.U.O. appears to be due to a pneumococcus affecting the mouth, nose and throat.

Besides the ordinary sanitary precautions, particular attention ~~should~~ will be paid to ventilation and units in huts should keep doors and windows <u>fully</u> open by day and night.

2. As a precaution, all ranks, whether sick or not, should use a mouth wash and gargle of potassium permanganate – 1 gr to 1 pint of water – at least three times a day.

Attention should also be paid to the cleanliness of the teeth. Medical Officers should arrange details as to method of issuing the mouth wash and times of using it with their C. O.

3. Severe cases of P.O.U.O. should be evacuated to Field Ambulances, milder cases, where units have huts, should be isolated from their Companies and treated regimentally in huts obtained from the unit for that purpose.

A J MacDougall

H.Q., 52nd Divn,
10th JUNE, 1918.

Colonel, A. M. S.,
A. D. M. S., 52nd (Lowland) Division

A.D.M.S., 52nd Divn. No. R.949/1.

July 1918.

A. D. M. S. 52nd Div.

Confidential.

War Diary

of

A.D.M.S. 52ND D.V.N.

FROM. :- 1ST. JULY TO

31ST. JULY 1918.

(VOLUME 7.)

Instructions regarding War Diaries and Intelligence Summaries are contained in F. S. Regs., Part II. and the Staff Manual respectively. Title pages will be prepared in manuscript.

WAR DIARY
or
~~INTELLIGENCE~~ SUMMARY.
(Erase heading not required.)

ADMS 52 Div JULY 1918

Army Form C. 2118.

Place	Date	Hour	Summary of Events and Information	Remarks and references to Appendices
CHATEAU D'ACQ	1.VII.18		Reported to Division the insanitary condition of HILLS CAMP especially with reference to latrines & cookhouses, the former are not fly proof & the latter are unserviceable & dirty.	
	2 VII.18		Reported on insanitary condition of OTTAWA camp the conditions much as in HILL CAMP	
			Orders from DDMS VIII Corps that cases of slight sickness & PUO up to 400 will be retained in FA of Division.	
	3.VII.18		Visited RISPIN & VILLERS Camp thorough reorganisation of the cookhouses of these camps is being carried out. Visited Divisional School of Cookery & gave lecture on Sanitation	
	4 VII.18		Conference with DDMS VIII Subject Sanitation & reports.	APPENDIX I MED. REPTS
	5 VII.18		Visited ADS & RAPS in left Section.	
	6 VII.18		Visited 1st & 3 Lowland FA. The 3 Lowland Fld on 2 VII 18 moved from their	

D. D. & L., London, E.C.
(A8104) Wt W1771/M2031 750,000 5/17 Sch. 52 Forms/C2118/14

Instructions regarding War Diaries and Intelligence Summaries are contained in F. S. Regs., Part II. and the Staff Manual respectively. Title pages will be prepared in manuscript.

WAR DIARY
or
INTELLIGENCE SUMMARY.
(Erase heading not required.)

Army Form C. 2118.

2

Place	Date	Hour	Summary of Events and Information	Remarks and references to Appendices
CHATEAU D'ACQ	6 VII	18	Site at AUX RIETZ to F9c near ST ELOI where new huts have been erected near the railway & a road made, 12 huts have been erected & others are in process of erection. The old main dressing station has been taken over by 1/2 [illegible] FA as a Walking Wounded Collecting Post.	A
	8 VII	18	Visited CAUCOURT & GAUCHIN LEGAL with a view to finding reserve sites for Field ambulances, at the former place there is a site in huts but the village is approach by only second class roads, it is in a hollow, & is difficult to approach or to evacuate from.	
			At GAUCHIN LEGAL there is a new Camp being erected, it has water, accommodation & easy approach, reported on sites to DDMS VIII Corps	
	9-VIII [illegible] 18		155 Brigade were relieved in the line by 156 Brigade Visited units in reserve at ST ELOI	
	10	VIII 18	Visited ADS & RAP in right section of Division	

D. D. & L., London, E.C.
(A8204) Wt W1771/M2031 750,000 5/17 Sch. 52 Forms/C2118/14

Instructions regarding War Diaries and Intelligence Summaries are contained in F. S. Regs., Part II. and the Staff Manual respectively. Title pages will be prepared in manuscript.

WAR DIARY
or
~~INTELLIGENCE SUMMARY.~~
(Erase heading not required.)

Army Form C. 2118.

3

Place	Date	Hour	Summary of Events and Information	Remarks and references to Appendices
CHATEAU D'ACQ	10 VII·18		As the epidemic of PUO has subsided recommended that gargling should be discontinued + concert halls reopened but that all doors + windows should be kept open + that gargling should continue in	
	11 VII·18		Visited DRR Disinfestors at BERTHONVAL + NEUVILLE ST WAAST, the disinfestor is in use at the latter place but owing to lack of thermometer, the work of the disinfestor in the former place is not satisfactory.	
			Visited Hills Camps, several sanitary improvements are being carried out	
	12 VII·18		Visited HANSON camp which is also being improved by the RE	
			Visited 52 Div MG Batt pointed out several defects to MO. The Battalion is moving to another site.	
			Visited Asst Director of light railways at BARLIN with a view to running hospital trains on the light line	
	13 VII·18		Visited 1/1 + 1/3 Lowland FA.	

D. D. & L., London, E.C. (A8104) Wt W1771/M2051 750,000 5/17 Sch. 52 Forms/C2118/14

Instructions regarding War Diaries and Intelligence Summaries are contained in F. S. Regs., Part II. and the Staff Manual respectively. Title pages will be prepared in manuscript.

WAR DIARY

or

~~INTELLIGENCE SUMMARY.~~

(Erase heading not required.)

Army Form C. 2118.

4

Place	Date	Hour	Summary of Events and Information	Remarks and references to Appendices
CHATEAU D'ACQ	14 VII 18		Infected men for reclassification	
	15 VII 18		4th Canadian Division took over part of the southern section of the Divisional front line from TIRED ALLEY to MERSEY ALLEY + CPR trench displacing 2 battalions of this Division. ADS in B2 + 94 is retained by this Division	
	16 VII 18		Proceeded to on 14 days leave handing over duty temporarily to Lt Col Keith DSO	
	17/7/18		Visited 1/1st Lowland F.A. + arranged that a new hut for use of dentist should be erected on ~~place~~ a site selected by me after consultation with the dental surgeon on 16/7/18 instead of making any attempt to repair the present one. Saw the Town major of VILLERS-AU-BOIS + arranged that the material of present hut should be used in the construction of the new one. Advised Major McKENZIE 1/1st Lowland F.A. that an officer R.E. would call on him at 9 A.M. to-morrow in accordance with arrangements to start with the work. [initials]	
	18/7/18		Visited 1/3rd L.F.A. main Dressing Station, 318th Road Construction Coy + Divisional	

D. D. & L., London, E.C.
(A8004) Wt W1771/M2031 750,000 5/17 Sch. 52 Forms/C2118/14

Instructions regarding War Diaries and Intelligence Summaries are contained in F. S. Regs., Part II. and the Staff Manual respectively. Title pages will be prepared in manuscript.

WAR DIARY

or

~~INTELLIGENCE SUMMARY.~~

(Erase heading not required.)

Army Form C. 2118.

A.D.M.S. 52nd Div JULY 1918 3.

Place	Date	Hour	Summary of Events and Information	Remarks and references to Appendices
CHATEAU D'ACQ	18/7/18		Gas Centre Baths. NEUVILLE ST. VAAST. The recent heavy rain has caused considerable damage to the recently erected huts one of which collapsed yesterday afternoon. The Verandah at the baths (Gas Centre) has not been erected yet by the R.E. nor have the doors into & out of the M.O.'s inspection room been made. Major BROWN D.A.D.M.S. saw the C.R.E. to-day on this subject & the work will be taken in hand immediately. Erection of new hut for dentist at 1/1st Lowland F.A. was commenced to-day. Received G. 3/1/3 d/18-7-18 "Very Secret" Warning Order that 52nd Div would be relieved by 6th Div. J.W.L.	
do.	19/7/18		~~A.D.M.S. [illegible]~~ Visited D.D.M.S. VIII Corps to ~~[illegible]~~ about matters connected with move.. J.W.L.	
do	20/7/18		A.D.M.S. 8th Div accompanied by D.A.D.M.S. 8th Div called at this office to-day & we arranged about the taking over of work & relief of ambulances. 1/2nd L.F.A. moved to-day to AUCHEL with 157th Bde Group. D.A.D.M.S. visited D.D.M.S. VIII & XVII Corps & most of the positions in new area which would be likely sites for Ambulances. leaving at 9 A.M. Visited Gas Centre & W.W.C.P. at AUX REITZ J.W.L. ~~Visited W.W.C.P. AUX~~	
do.	21/7/18		Issued R.A.M.C. Operation Orders No 6 (see APPENDIX. II). ~~REITZ to see Major LAMB 1/2nd L.F.A. who has been left~~ Major LAMB 1/2nd L.F.A. & his party proceeded to join his unit at AUCHEL to-day after completing	APPENDIX II

D. D. & L., London, E.C. (A8203) Wt W1771/M2031 750,000 5/17 Sch. 52 Forms/C2118/14

Instructions regarding War Diaries and Intelligence Summaries are contained in F. S. Regs., Part II. and the Staff Manual respectively. Title pages will be prepared in manuscript.

WAR DIARY
~~or~~
~~INTELLIGENCE SUMMARY.~~
(Erase heading not required.)

Army Form C. 2118.

ADMS. ...
52nd Division

6

Place	Date	Hour	Summary of Events and Information	Remarks and references to Appendices
CHATEAU D'ACQ	21/7/18 (Contd)		the work of handing over W.W.C.P. & Gas Centre to officer of 24th F.A. sent to take over. Visited 1/1st L.F.A. where new hut for use of dentist is now nearly erected. J.W.L.	
do.	22/7/18.		1/1st L.F.A. was relieved at VILLERS-AU-BOIS last night by 25th F.A. & proceeded by road to-day to near BARLIN with 156th Bde Group. 1/3rd L.F.A. was relieved to-day at MONT St ELOY by 26th F.A. & proceeded to FRESNICOURT with 155th Bde Group. Visited PERNES to-day by ambulance car accompanied by ~~Capt.~~ Major BROWN, DADMS. Visited 1/2nd L.F.A. at AUCHEL where there is accommodation for 50 cases in building near HOTEL DE VILLE; & also sites allotted for billets to 1/1st LFA at FOSSE 9 (1½ miles S. of BARLIN), & to 1/3rd L.F.A. in FRESNICOURT. There is no suitable Hospital accommodation at either of the latter two places. I advised that the tents of 1 section should be used by these ambulances for reception of sick for evacuation. A.D.M.S. 1st DIVISION has kindly arranged to receive any sick at ambulance of that Division stationed in BARLIN if called upon. J.W.L.	
do.	23/7/18.		Handed over to D.A.D.M.S. 8th Division at 9-30 A.M. this morning & left with remainder of office staff for D.H.Q. at PERNES. at 10-5 A.M. J.W.L.	

D. D. & L., London, E.C.
(A8204) Wt W1771/M2031 750,000 5/17 Sch. 52 Forms/C2118/14

Army Form C. 2118.

Instructions regarding War Diaries and Intelligence Summaries are contained in F. S. Regs., Part II. and the Staff Manual respectively. Title pages will be prepared in manuscript.

WAR DIARY
~~or~~
~~INTELLIGENCE SUMMARY.~~
(Erase heading not required.)

A.D.M.S.
52nd Division.

7

Place	Date	Hour	Summary of Events and Information	Remarks and references to Appendices
PERNES	23/7/18.	10pm	Arrived at new quarters (Billet 127) about 11-30 a.m., Heavy rain throughout the day. Called at HQ 52nd M.G. Batt, with a view to getting aid post there in which the M.O. i/c could see the sick of ~~A~~ Cy M.G. Batt. & also any sick of Divisional troops in PERNES other than those of D.H.Q.; aid POST for D.H.Q. has been arranged at Billet 148 at N. exit from the town on road to AUCHEL. JWL	
Do.	24/7/18		Issued instructions to M.O. i/c 17th NORTUMBERLAND FUSILIERS (Pioneer Batt) at TANGRY ~~&~~ to M.O. i/c 52nd D.A.C. to send wire to this office daily by 11 a.m. stating numbers requiring evacuation to Hospital (SR 143/11 of even date). An ambulance motor from 1/2nd L.F.A. will be stationed in Square at PERNES to collect these cases & take them to 1/2nd L.F.A. in AUCHEL. Instructed Fld Ambulances that cases for examination by Eye Specialist would be sent to 1/2nd L.F.A. on previous evening for evacuation by 9 A.M. on Thursdays (for men) + Saturdays (for officers): while cases for Ear & Throat & Nose Specialists would be ~~collected by~~ sent to 1/3rd L.F.A. at FRESNICOURT on previous evening ~~by~~ for ~~[illegible]~~ purpose of being sent to ST POL by 9 A.M. on Thursdays for men & Saturdays for officers. (R 1526/7). Instructed O.C. 1/3rd L.F.A. to evacuate cases from 9th Bde R.F.A., ~~[illegible]~~ telegram from M.O. i/c 9th Bde to be	

D. D. & L., London, E.C. (A8204) Wt W1771/M2031 750,000 5/17 Sch. 52 Forms/C2118/14

Instructions regarding War Diaries and Intelligence Summaries are contained in F. S. Regs., Part II. and the Staff Manual respectively. Title pages will be prepared in manuscript.

WAR DIARY

~~or~~

~~INTELLIGENCE SUMMARY.~~

(Erase heading not required.)

Army Form C. 2118.

ADMS. 52nd Division

8

Place	Date	Hour	Summary of Events and Information	Remarks and references to Appendices
PERNES	24/7/18. (Contd.)		sent to O.C. 1/3rd L.F.A. through 155th Bde HQ by 11 a.m. stating numbers (if any) requiring evacuation. (R 1524/7 of even date). Visited HQ 155 Bde in VERDREL & HQ 156th Bde in BARLIN re Baths for the men. Arrangements have been made for 100 men per day from 156th Bde to have hot bath & change of clothing at Baths in BARLIN. Arrangements are to be made for 1/4th RSF (155th Bde) in VERDREL to have hot bath & disinfection of clothing at Baths in BARLIN. & for 50 men per day of the 2 other Battns of this Bde stationed in CAMBLAIN L'ABBE to have hot bath at De La HAIE (60th Fld. Amb.) if coal can be provided by this (52nd) Division. Visited also 1/1st LFA at Cité Jeanne D'ARC & 1/3rd L.F.A. at FRESNICOURT & called on O.C. 1st Fld Amb. 1st Division in BARLIN. Learned that 1st Fld Amb. did not keep any cases in BARLIN but evacuated them to 3rd Amb. M.D.S. at RUITZ (2nd Fld Amb. 1st Division) JWL.	
do	25/7/18		Visited 157th Bde HQ at AUCHEL. There are no hot baths obtainable for men in this area but it has been arranged that Bde Group can have sole use of cold shower baths ~~[illegible]~~ for 5 days in week including Sunday. The accommodation at these baths is 300 per day + 700 on Sunday & they are at the mines & supplied by water pumped up by engine power at the mines. 1900 men per week will thus obtain a bath, but there are no facilities for disinfection of clothing. This, however,	

D. D. & L., London, E.C. (A8004) Wt W1771/M2031 750,000 5/17 Sch. 52 Forms/C2118/14

Instructions regarding War Diaries and Intelligence Summaries are contained in F. S. Regs., Part II. and the Staff Manual respectively. Title pages will be prepared in manuscript.

WAR DIARY

or

~~INTELLIGENCE SUMMARY.~~

(Erase heading not required.)

Army Form C. 2118.

A.D.M.S. 52nd Division

9.

Place	Date	Hour	Summary of Events and Information	Remarks and references to Appendices
PERNES	25/7/18 (Contd.)		is not a matter of immediate urgency as 157th Bde was in reserve up to time of move & whole Bde had had bath & disinfection of clothing at Divisional Baths at BERTHONVAL FARM. In afternoon visited D.A.C. at OURTON & 56th Bde RFA in BOIS DE HAZOIS. The latter are living in the woods & conditions not very satisfactory. Arranged that sick for evacuation would be taken to D.A.C. Aid Post in OURTON where an ambulance motor would be sent daily at 11 a.m. to move sick to 1/2nd L.F.A. It was found necessary to fall back on this original arrangement as these units have no means of sending a wire to Division H.Q. except by circuitous route.	J.W.L.
do	26/7/18		Visited Train H.Q. at PRESSY LE PERNES & arranged with O.C. Train to have superstructure for carrying petrol tins for storage of water fitted to the water carts of the Ambulances by the A.S.C. Coy in each Bde group. Issued instructions to O.C. Fd Ambulances re dental arrangements – each ambulance to send 5 cases from respective Bde Groups every 4th day (excluding Sundays) to C.C.S. AUBIGNY by ambulance motor.	J.W.L.
do	27/7/18		56th Bde R.F.A. moved to DIVION yesterday. Instructed ambulance motor car which goes daily from this office at 11 A.M. to 52nd D.A.C. at OURTON to return via DIVION & collect any sick from 56th Bde RFA in future. Dental cases sent to 57th C.C.S. by 1/2nd L.F.A. were returned untreated as C.C.S. was on the move.	J.W.L.

D. D. & L., London, E.C. (A8204) Wt W1771/M2031 750,000 5/17 Sch. 52 Forms/C2118/14

Instructions regarding War Diaries and Intelligence Summaries are contained in F. S. Regs., Part II. and the Staff Manual respectively. Title pages will be prepared in manuscript.

WAR DIARY
or
~~INTELLIGENCE SUMMARY.~~
(Erase heading not required.)

Army Form C. 2118.

A.D.M.S.
52nd Division

10

Place	Date	Hour	Summary of Events and Information	Remarks and references to Appendices
PERNES.	28/7/18.		Visited the G.O.C. Division for usual weekly interview on medical matters. Brought to his notice the facts contained in my letter R1583/7 d/28th which I was sending to D.H.Q. viz. (1) the advantage of having accommodation for light sick cases as shown by numbers retained in, & evacuated by, 1/2 L.F.A. (which had good billets for 50 sick) as compared with 1/1st L.F.A. & 1/3rd L.F.A. where billets for sick were not available & only a few tents could be erected owing to the tactical necessity of avoiding aerial observation; (2) the likelihood of a serious increase in numbers of sick suffering from rheumatism, fevers, bowel complaints among troops of 156th Bde in BOIS DE OLHAIN & 56th Bde R.F.A. in BOIS DE HAZOIS on account of the wet condition of the ground on which their tents & bivouacs were, owing to the recent heavy rains. In afternoon attended at medical inspection room of 1st Army Artillery School & Reinforcement Camp, VERCHIN; ~~examined 18 O.R. with submitted for reclassification~~ in accordance with D.D.M.S.'s instructions & examined 18 O.R. submitted for reclassification. Recommended 4 to be sent to Base for re-classification & for reclassification. Sent letter to DDMS reporting accordingly. J.W.L.	
PERNES	29/7/18		Received Wires G.A. 411 & G.A. 414 d/29/7/18 stating that 17th Corps would relieve Canadian Corps in ARRAS sector of the line, Infantry relief to commence night 31st July/1st Aug.	

D. D. & L., London, E.C.
(A8004) Wt W1771/M2031 750,000 5/17 Sch. 52 Forms/C2118/14

Instructions regarding War Diaries and Intelligence Summaries are contained in F. S. Regs., Part II. and the Staff Manual respectively. Title pages will be prepared in manuscript.

WAR DIARY
~~or~~
~~INTELLIGENCE SUMMARY.~~
(Erase heading not required.)

Army Form C. 2118.

A.D.M.S.
52nd Division

11

Place	Date	Hour	Summary of Events and Information	Remarks and references to Appendices
PERNES	29/7/18 (Contd)		Proceeded to H.Q. 4th Canadian Division at MAROEUIL accompanied by DADMS & arranged provisionally with ADMS to take over M.D.S. & A.D.S. & posts in forward area & Div. Rest station occupied by ambulances of 4th Canadian Division. JWL	
do	30/7/18		Received 52nd Div order No 118 d/29/7/18 early this morning & issued RAMC O.O. No 7 d/30/7/18 (see APPENDIX) embodying the arrangements provisionally come to with A.D.M.S. 4th Canadian Division. In 52nd Div. order No 118 showed that this Division was not taking over the right section of 4th Canadian Divisional front. I proceeded again to MAROEUIL accompanied by D.A.D.M.S. & was fortunate to meet A.D.M.S. 57th Division at office of A.D.M.S. 4th Canadian Division in process of arranging to take over the A.D.S. & posts serving the right section of the line held by 4th Canadian Division. We both (A.D.M.S. 57th Div & myself) proceeded to see D.D.M.S. XVII Corps at C.H.Q., DUISANS, & I received instructions from him to take over M.D.S. at MAROEUIL & corresponding A.D.S. & posts, H.Q. of [illegible] Field Amb at ECOIVRES, & Divisional Rest Station at AUBIGNY. Saw O.C. Field ambulances concerned, returned to PERNES & issued to all concerned Amendment to RAMC O.O. No 7 d/30/7/18 (See APPENDIX) JWL	APPENDIX III APPENDIX IV.
do	31/7/18		Ambulances have now all moved to new area & are located as follows:- 1/1st L.F.A.	

D. D. & L., London, E.C. (A8004) Wt W1771/M2031 750,000 5/17 Sch. 52 Forms/C2118/14

Army Form C. 2118.

WAR DIARY
or
INTELLIGENCE SUMMARY.
(Erase heading not required.)

Instructions regarding War Diaries and Intelligence Summaries are contained in F. S. Regs., Part II. and the Staff Manual respectively. Title pages will be prepared in manuscript.

A.D.M.S. 52nd Division 12

Place	Date	Hour	Summary of Events and Information	Remarks and references to Appendices
PERNES.			at ECOIVRES, F.13.a.8.2.; 1/2nd L.F.A at MAROEUIL (L.4.a.4.6 Sheet 51B) and A.28.a.7.6., Sheet 51B., (A.D.S., LENS ROAD); 1/3rd L.F.A at AUBIGNY; E.1.c.4.4, Sheet 51C (Divisional Rest station).	
			John M. Leitch Lt Col. A/A.D.M.S. 52nd Divn.	

D. D. & L., London, E.C. (A8094) Wt W1771/M2031 750,000 5/17 Sch. 52 Forms/C2118/14

Appendix I

Copy No. 15

SECRET

SUMMARY OF MEDICAL ARRANGEMENTS 52nd (Lowland) DIVISION.

4th JULY, 1918.

Reference:- Map - Army Map "B", 1/40,000

1. LOCATIONS.

A.D.M.S. Office :- CHATEAU ACQ - W.30.b.4.5.
1st Low. Fld. Amb.:- Divisional Rest Station - VILLERS AU BOIS - X.19.c.9.9.
2nd Low. Fld. Amb.:- Main Dressing Station - LES 4 VENTS - W.9.d.1.9.
Walking Wounded Collecting Post - AUX RIETZ - A.8.c.5.5.
3rd Low. Fld. Amb.:- Main Dressing Station - MONT ST ELOI - F.9.c.
Advanced Dressing Stations -
LA CHAUDIERE - S.18.c.9.3.
FARBUS -------- B.2.a.9.4.

Regimental Aid Posts.	Relay Posts.
T.13.b.5.4.	T.15.a.5.5.
T.21.a.2.0.	T.20.b.2.8.
T.19.c.2.5.	T.26.a.2.9.
T.28.a.4.1.	T.26.d.9.7.
T.26.d.9.7.	T.27.d.2.4.
B.9.a.8.7.	T.19.c.2.5.
	B.2.d.3.5.
	A.11.b.3.9.

Detraining Centre -------------V.29.a.75.55.(near MINGOVAL)
Car Relay Posts ---------------T.25.a.9.4. and F.8.c.9.4.
Gas Centre --------------------A.9.a.5.5.(Baths-NEUVILLE ST VAAST.)

2. WOUNDED.

Normally, all wounded will pass through the A.D.Ss whence they will be evacuated by Motor Ambulance Cars of the Field Ambulance to the M.D.S., at F.9.c., from which they will be evacuated by M.A.C. Cars.

3. SICK.

Sick of Units in the trenches will be evacuated through A.D.Ss to M.D.S., F.9.c. and either evacuated, retained, or sent to the Divisional Rest Station according to the case.
Sick of Units in NEUVILLE ST VAAST Area will be admitted to the Walking Wounded Collecting Post and thence transferred to M.D.S. and LES 4 VENTS. O.C., Field Ambulance at LES 4 VENTS will be responsible for collection of sick requiring transport.
O.C., Divisional Rest Station will collect sick from the Brigade in Reserve at ST ELOI. One ambulance car will be kept by this unit at ST ELOI (near the Baths) for emergency cases.

4. WALKING WOUNDED.

During heavy fighting, when there are numbers of walking wounded, those will be evacuated to Walking Wounded Collecting Post and thence to Detraining Centre by Light Railway or Motor Lorry, or other means as directed.

5. GASSED CASES.

Severe cases will be evacuated to C.C.S. from the M.D.S. at F.9.c.
Slight and doubtful cases will be transferred from the M.D.S. at F.9.c. to the Divisional Rest Station.

ACKNOWLEDGE.

A.J. MacDougall
Colonel, A. M. S.,
A. D. M. S., 52nd (Lowland) Division.

SECRET.

ADDENDUM TO MEDICAL ARRANGEMENTS IN THE EVENT OF A HOSTILE ATTACK - 52nd DIVISION.

Insert - Para.2 (c)

M.O.i/c, Divisional [illegible] and M.O.i/c, 52nd D.A.C. will report for duty at M.D.S., F.O.c. M.O.i/c, 52nd Bn.M.G.C. will report for duty at the W.W.C.P.

Colonel, A.M.S.,
A.D.M.S., 52nd (Lowland) Division.

H.Q., 52nd Divn.
4th JULY, 1918.

Copies to all recipients of original arrangements.

SECRET.

Copy No. 15

MEDICAL ARRANGEMENTS
52nd (LOWLAND) DIVISION
IN THE EVENT OF A HOSTILE ATTACK.

1. EVACUATION. (a) In the event of active operations, stretcher and
sitting cases will be evacuated from A.D.S. to M.D.S. at
F.9.c. and walking cases to Walking Wounded Collecting Post
at AUX RIETZ (A.8.c.5.5.) Cases will be collected by hand
carry, wheeled stretchers, ambulance cars and wagons, tram
trollies and light railway, according to circumstances.
O.C., M.D.S. at F.9.c. is responsible for making
arrangements for trains between A.D.S. and M.D.S.
(b) Stretcher and sitting cases will be evacuated from the
M.D.S. at F.9.c. by M.A.C. cars.
(c) Walking Wounded will be evacuated from the W.W.C.P.
to Detraining Centre at V.29.a.75.35.(near MINGOVAL) by means
of the Light Railway. O.C., W.W.C.P. will be responsible
for making arrangements for trains on the light railway
between W.W.C.P. and Detraining Centre. All applications
for trains will be made to TRAFFIC CONTROL, ZIVY.
An N.C.O. and orderly will accompany each train to the
Detraining Centre. They will be in charge of the patients
and will be responsible for their comfort. On detrainment,
they will report to the O.C., Detraining Centre who will
arrange for their return to the W.W.C.P. in the most
expeditious manner, either by returning train or by M.A.C.
cars returning from the C.C.S. Each patient will have a
blanket and, in wet weather, a waterproof sheet, which,
on detraining, will be collected and returned to W.W.C.P.
by the O.C., Detraining Centre in the most expeditious
manner as in the case of orderlies.
A detraining party will be detailed (as below) and four
motor lorries will be supplied by Corps for removing cases
from the Detraining Centre to the C.C.S.
<u>NO</u> stretcher cases will be evacuated by the train
from the W.W.C.P.
One motor lorry and one ambulance car will be on duty
at the W.W.C.P., the former for evacuation of cases to the
C.C.S. which, on its return, will call at the Detraining
Centre and bring back any orderlies or equipment that may be
there for return to the W.W.C.P. The ambulance car will be
used for any cases requiring removal as stretcher cases.
(d) Sick cases will be sent to the M.D.S. at F.9.c. and
thence by M.A.C. to C.C.S. Slight cases will be sent to
the Divisional Rest Station.

2. PERSONNEL. (a) O.C., Field Ambulance at LES 4 VENTS will detail two
officers and all his bearers to report to O.C., Field Amb.
at M.D.S., F.9.c. who will reinforce his bearer sub-divisions
as necessary.
(b) O.C., Fld. Amb. conducting the Divisional Rest Station
will detail an officer with 1 N.C.O. and 9 privates for duty
at the Detraining Centre with equipment already detailed.
He will hold his bearer sub-divisions in readiness to
reinforce as ordered. He will order an officer to proceed
to Forward Battle Stragglers Collecting Station, A.11.a.0.8.
(Divnl Administrative Instructions No. A.F.9.)

3. TRANSPORT. Ambulance cars will be used for evacuation in the Divisional Area/

Area and will not proceed to the C.C.S. without orders from th this office.

Ten M.A.C. Cars will evacuate from the M.D.S. and F.9.c.

O.C., Divnl Rest Station will place his ambulance motor cars at the disposal of O.C., M.D.S., F.9.c.

O.C., Fld. Amb. at LES 4 VENTS will detail one car for duty at the W.W.C.P. and will hold the remainder in reserve.

Two horsed ambulances from O.C., Divisional Rest Station will be at the disposal of the O.C., M.D.S.,F.9.c. to convey cases to the Divisional Rest Station.

Car Relay Posts between the A.D.S. and M.D.S. will be arranged by O.C., M.D.S., F.9.c.

All drivers of cars will have precise orders in writing as to where they are to go and return.

4. MEDICAL.

(a) Anti-tetanic serum will be given in all cases at the A.D.S. A check will be made at the M.D.S. and any case who has not had A.T.S. will be given it before evacuation.

(b) Dressings may be obtained, if necessary, on urgent indent direct on No. 33 Advanced Depot of Medical Stores, SAVY, two copies of the indent being subsequently sent to this office.

(c) Os.C., Fld. Ambulancesnwill indent direct on S.S.O. for food and medical comforts for patients.

5. GENERAL.

All changes in the positions of A.D.Ss, R.A.Ps and Relay Posts will be reported to this office at once.

Applications for bearers, cars etc will be made to this office.

Attention is called to D.D.M.S., No. 2999, Summary of Medical Arrangements, XVIII Corps, in the event of a Hostile Attack.

A. J. MacDougall

Colonel, A. M. S.,
A. D. M. S., 52nd (Lowland) Division.

****

Copy No. 1 to 1/1st Lowland Field Ambulance.
2 1/2nd Lowland Field Ambulance.
3 1/3rd Lowland Field Ambulance.
4 "G"
5 "A" and "Q"
6 D.D.M.S., VIII Corps.
7 A.D.M.S., 20th Divn.
8 A.D.M.S., 24th Divn.
9 A.D.M.S., 51st Divn.
10 H.Q., 155 Inf. Bde.
11 H.Q., 156 Inf. Bde.
12 H.Q., 157 Inf. Bde.
13 C. R. A., 52nd Divn.
14 Diary.
15 Diary. ✓
16 File.

****

Appendix II

1 O.C. 1st [illegible]
2 O.C. 2nd [illegible]
3 O.C. 3rd [illegible]

Copy to :-

4 Headquarters, [illegible] Brigade.
5 Headquarters, [illegible] Brigade.
6 Headquarters, [illegible] Brigade.
7 C. R. A. 52nd Division.
8 A.D.M.S. 6th Division.
9 H.Q.R.A. XVIII Corps.
10-11 Diary.
12 File.

13 ADMS XVII Corps
14 AHQ

Copy 10 SR 143/15

[illegible]

Lieut-Colonel [illegible]
A.D.M.S. [illegible] (Lowland) Division [illegible]

Reference [illegible]
[illegible]
Ref. 52nd Division [illegible] and [illegible]

1. [illegible].
[illegible] Division will be relieved by [illegible] relief will move to [illegible] Reserve under administration of [illegible]. During the move Field Ambulances will come under administration of G.O.Cs Brigades as follows :-
1/1st Lowland Field Ambulance = G.O.C. [illegible] Brigade.
1/2nd Lowland Field Ambulance = G.O.C. 157th Brigade.
1/3rd Lowland Field Ambulance = G.O.C. 156th Brigade.

2. MOVES. 1/1st Lowland Field Ambulance will be relieved at [illegible] on 21st instant by [illegible] Field Ambulance and will move on [illegible] to neighbourhood of [illegible] under orders of G.O.C. [illegible] Brigade. Relief to be completed by [illegible] on 21st instant.

1/2nd Lowland Field Ambulance moved on [illegible] to [illegible] under orders of G.O.C. 157th Brigade and was relieved by [illegible] Field Ambce.

1/3rd Lowland Field Ambulance will be relieved at [illegible] and Posts in Forward Area by [illegible] Field Ambulance on [illegible].
All reliefs to be completed by midnight [illegible]/23rd instant.
1/3rd L.F.A. on relief will move to neighbourhood of [illegible] under orders of G.O.C. 156th Brigade.

3. EVACUATION. Sick or wounded not evacuated will be transferred to relieving Field Ambulance.
In new Area evacuation will be to receiving [illegible] from 1/1st and 1/2nd Lowland Field Ambulances by motor ambulances of these units concerned.
1/3rd L.F.A. will similarly evacuate to receiving [illegible].
Until further orders evacuation of cases to [illegible] or [illegible] Specialist or Dentist will be suspended.
1/1st L.F.A. will evacuate sick from [illegible] in addition to those of Brigade Group.
1/2nd L.F.A. will similarly evacuate sick from [illegible] Company (not [illegible] Company) [illegible] Battalion and from Divisional Artillery in accordance with this Office [illegible] 143/11 dated [illegible].
1/3rd L.F.A. will similarly evacuate sick from [illegible].

4. A.D.M.S. Office will close at [illegible] and will open at [illegible] same hour.

5. ACKNOWLEDGE.

[signature] Lieut-Colonel.
A/A.D.M.S. 52nd Division.

(c) 52nd D.A.C. moves to OURTON on 21st instant and 56th Bde R.F.A
to BOIS de HAZOIS (LENS Edition 2 F.1.9.4.) on 22nd instant.

157 Brigade Group.
52nd D.A.C.
MEDICAL ARRANGEMENTS FOR :- 58th Bde. R.F.A.
'C' Coy. M.G.Bn.

---

1. EVACUATIONS WITHIN THE DIVISIONAL AREA.

(a) Sick and wounded of 157 Brigade Group and 'A' Company M.G.Battalion will be admitted by you forthwith.

(b) 'C' Company M.G.Bn moves to PERNES on 23nd instant and from then will have any sick evacuated by you. ~~and 58th Bde R.F.A. to BOIS de NAZOIS (LENS Edition 8 P.1.C.4.) on 22nd instant.~~

(c) X One Motor Ambulance will be sent daily at 11 a.m. to report to M.O.i/c 52nd D.A. . who will have cases from 58th Brigade R.F.A. and 52nd D.A.C. ready for evacuation to your unit by this Car.

(d) Any cases likely to be fit in 4 days should be detained in your Ambulance if accommodation is sufficient.

11. EVACUATIONS OUTWITH THE DIVISIONAL AREA.

(a) All cases other than those for Special Hospitals will be sent to the receiving C. .Ss in PERNES by your motor amb lances.

(b) Cases to be evacuated to Special Hospitals will be sent ~~xxxxxx~~ by your own Motor Ambulances and not by M.A.C.

Cases for EYE, Ear, Nose and throat Specialists' opinion will not be sent till further orders.

111. RETURNS. You will continue to send to this Office and at the same hours the returns (except mid day returns) at present being rendered.

1V. MOVE. A.D.M.S. Office will close at CHATEAU D'ACQ at noon and reopen at PERNES same hour on 23rd instant.

V. General. Telephonic communication with this Office may be obtained through Headquarters 157 Infantry Brigade.

20 / 7 / 18. Si ned (Lieut-Colonel), J.W. Leitch.

A / A.D.M.S. 52nd Division.

Copies to

O.C. 2nd L. F. A.
C.R.A. for D.A.C. and 58th Bde R.F.A.
Headquarters 157th Bde.
M.G.Bn.
File.
DIARY.

) X Commencing 22nd instant.

Appendix III

Secret Copy No

R.A.M.C. OPERATION ORDER No. 7. 30th, JULY, 1918.
BY
Lieut-Colonel J.W.LEITCH, D.S.O.
A/A.D.M.S. 52nd.Div.

Reference Map - LENS 11, 1/100,000.
" 52nd Division Order No.118 dated 29/7/18.

1. INFORMATION. 52nd Division will relieve a portion of 4th Canadian Division in the line from TOWEY ALLEY at H.5.a.7.6. inclusive to WESTERN ROAD (Corps Northern Boundary) on July 31st and succeeding days.

2. MOVES. 1/1st Lowland Field Ambulance, which moves with 156th Brigade to MAROEUIL Area on 30th instant, will relieve 13th Canadian Field Ambulance at 3.J.3.6. (ST.CATHERINE) and posts occupied by them in the Forward Area.
Reliefs to be completed by 6 p.m. on 31st July.

1/2nd Lowland Field Ambulance, which moves with 157th Bde., will relieve the 12th Canadian Field Ambulance near AGNEZ LES DUISANS, 3.I.1.8. (road 1 mile north east of A in AGNEZ) and will form the Divisional Rest Station.
Relief to be completed by 6 p.m. on 1st August.

1/3rd Lowland Field Ambulance, which moves with 155th Bde., will relieve the 11th Canadian Field Ambulance at M.D.S. at MAROEUIL 3.I.5.8. and posts held by them in the forward area.
Reliefs to be completed by 6 p.m. on 31st July.

3. EVACUATION. Maps of Area and details of present scheme of evacuation will be handed over by Canadian Field Ambulances to relieving Field Ambulances.
Cases likely to be fit in 7 to 10 days and cases of Skin Disease and uncomplicated Scabies will be sent to Divisional Rest Station.

4. REPORTS. Completion of moves report will be wired to A.D.M.S. 52nd Division.
A.D.M.S. Office will close at PERNES 10 a.m. on 2nd August and will open same hour at MAROEUIL

5. ACKNOWLEDGE

Lieut-Colonel,
A./A. D. M. S. 52nd Division.

Copies to :-
1. 1st L.F.A.
2. 2nd L.F.A.
3. 3rd L.F.A.
4. A.D.M.S. 4th Canadian Div.
5. A.D.M.S. 57th Division.
6. A.D.M.S. 8th Division.
7. D.D.M.S. XVII Corps.
8. H.Q. 52nd Div.
9. 155 Inf.Bde.
10. 156 Inf.Bde.
11. 157 Inf.Bde.
12 & 13 Diary.
14 F I L E.

Diary. Appendix IV. Secret

AMENDMENT TO R.A.M.C.OPERATION ORDER No 7.
By
Lieut-Colonel J.W. Leitch, D.S.O.
A/A.D.M.S. 52nd Division. 30th July 1918.

Cancel paragraph 2 and substitute :-

"2. MOVES. 1/1st Lowland Field Ambulance will take over the Headquarters of the 13th Canadian Field Ambulance, ECOIVRES on 31st.

1/2nd Lowland Field Ambulance will move to MAROEUIL on the 31st and will relieve the 11th Canadian Field Ambulance at M.D.S. 3.I.5.8. and posts held by them in the Forward Area.
Reliefs to be completed by noon on the 1st prox.

1/3rd Lowland Field Ambulance will relieve the 2/2nd London Field Ambulance at AUBIGNY and occupy their Camp, E.1.c.4.4. as the Divisional Rest Station.
Relief to be completed ON 31st instant.

Copies to all recipients of R.A.M.C.O.O.No.7.

John W. Leitch Lieut-Colonel.
A. / A.D.M.S, 52nd Division.

Confidential

War Diary

of

A.D.M.S. 52nd DIVISION.

1st to 31st AUGUST, 1918.

(VOLUME 8.)

Instructions regarding War Diaries and Intelligence Summaries are contained in F. S. Regs., Part II. and the Staff Manual respectively. Title pages will be prepared in manuscript.

WAR DIARY

~~or~~

~~INTELLIGENCE SUMMARY.~~

(Erase heading not required.)

Army Form C. 2118.

1

Place	Date	Hour	Summary of Events and Information	Remarks and references to Appendices
Pernes	1/8/18		1/2 L. F. Ambce moved from Auchel and relieved 11th Canadian F. Ambce in M.D.S. at Moroeuil, A.D.S at Ecoivres and various relay posts in the line. All evacuations from front line units done through this M.D.S. 1/1 L.F.A now located in Ecoivres & admitting sick transferred from 1/2 L.F.A, also from units in Ecoivres area. 1/3 L.F.A now located at Aubigny & acting as D.R.S. A.D.M.S. returned from leave today	
MAROEUIL	2/8/18		52nd D.H.Q. moved from Pernes, & occupied site vacated by 4th Canadn Division at MAROEUIL	
	3/8/18		Visited M.D.S. and A.D.S of 1/2 L.F.A	
	4/8/18		Visited Regimental aid posts in TUNNEL.	

D. D. & L., London, E.C.
(A8004) Wt W177/M2031 750,000 5/17 Sch. 52 Forms/C2118/13

Instructions regarding War Diaries and Intelligence Summaries are contained in F. S. Regs., Part II. and the Staff Manual respectively. Title pages will be prepared in manuscript.

WAR DIARY

~~or~~

~~INTELLIGENCE SUMMARY.~~

(Erase heading not required.)

Army Form C. 2118.

2

Place	Date	Hour	Summary of Events and Information	Remarks and references to Appendices
MARDEUIL	5.8.15		Visited 1/1 Lowland FA & Divisional Reception Camps pointed out various insanitary conditions left by former unit & made recommendations for their removal	
"	6.8.15		2 American officers joined for duty Visited Regimental aid posts on ~~left~~ right of line	
"	7.8.15		Visited DDMS XVII Corps at his office, he having been out at my first visit Met DMS 1st Army at the Divisional Rest Station	
"	8.8.15		Visited 1/1 Lowland FA & Nucleus camp of 156 Brigade pointed out various insanitary conditions	
"	9.8.15		Visited Regimental aid post on left of line Reported to Division generally unsatisfactory condition of latrine trenches in line, especially one in BRIERLY TRENCH	

D. D. & L., London, E.C.
(A8104) Wt W1771/M2031 750,000 5/14 Sch. 52 Forms/C2118/14

Instructions regarding War Diaries and Intelligence Summaries are contained in F. S. Regs., Part II. and the Staff Manual respectively. Title pages will be prepared in manuscript.

WAR DIARY
or
~~INTELLIGENCE SUMMARY.~~
(Erase heading not required.)

Army Form C. 2118.

8

Place	Date	Hour	Summary of Events and Information	Remarks and references to Appendices
MAROEUIL	9.8.18		which had been reported by me on the 5th as being insanitary & not fly proof	
	10.8.18		Visited Camp of 17 Northumberland Fusiliers (Pioneer battalion)	
			3 officers & 3 other ranks American Army joined for 4 days instruction in front line work	
	11.8.18		1st Army RAMC school of instruction commenced class 3 officers + 6 OR attended a course finishing on 24th	
	12.8.18		Visited Baths at MAROEUIL + ECUIRE	
	13.8.18		Visited RAP at TUNNEL + Relay post at CUTTING. Defective latrine in BRIERLY TRENCH reported by me on 5th + 9th still defective, wrote to DHQ on this matter + general state of sanitation	
			Capt RM ROSS RAMC TC reported for duty	
	14.8.18		Shell landed last night in MDS of 1/2 Lowland Fld Ambulance + set on fire one ambulance car damaged another 6 wounded 4 of whom are at duty.	

D. D. & L., London, E.C.
(A8204) Wt W1771/M2031 750,000 5/17 Sch. 52 Forms/C2118/14

Instructions regarding War Diaries and Intelligence Summaries are contained in F. S. Regs., Part II. and the Staff Manual respectively. Title pages will be prepared in manuscript.

WAR DIARY

or

~~INTELLIGENCE SUMMARY.~~

(Erase heading not required.)

Army Form C. 2118.

4

Place	Date	Hour	Summary of Events and Information	Remarks and references to Appendices
Maroeuil	15/8/18		Operation Order No 8 issued.	Appendix I
			155 Bde relieved in the line and now located in Ecoivres - St Eloy area	
			Sick from this Bde admitted by 1/1 L. F.A.	
			Relay Posts of R. Bde in line handed over to 1/2 Highland Field Ambce	
	16/8/18		156 Bde relieved in the line and moved into Savy Area.	
			Sick from this brigade to be sent to 1/3 L.F.A at Aubigny	
			~~Rel~~ A.D.S. at Ecoivres and Relay Posts of Left and Centre Brigades handed over to 26th F Ambce of 8th Division at midnight	
			52 D. Artillery now moved to Acq. 1/1 L.F.A ordered to collect any sick till they move on 19th inst. 52 D.H.Q. closed at 9am today, & reopened at Villers Chatel same hour	
Villers Chatel	17/8/18		1/2 L.F.A relieved in MDS at Maroeuil by 1/3 Highland F. Ambce and moved to new site in Gouy-Servins Q36d. vacated by 1/3 H. F Ambce	
			157 Bde now moved from line to Ecoivres St Eloy area.	
			1/1 L.F.A ordered to collect sick from this Bde	
	18/8/18		155 Bde moved from Ecoivres - St Eloy area to Caucourt - Hermin - Gauchin Legal area, 1/1 L.F.A. still collecting their sick	

D. D. & L., London, E.C.
(A8204) Wt W1771/M2031 750,000 5/17 Sch. 58 Forms/C2118/14

Instructions regarding War Diaries and Intelligence Summaries are contained in F. S. Regs., Part II. and the Staff Manual respectively. Title pages will be prepared in manuscript.

WAR DIARY

~~or~~

~~INTELLIGENCE SUMMARY.~~

(Erase heading not required.)

Army Form C. 2118.

5

Place	Date	Hour	Summary of Events and Information	Remarks and references to Appendices
~~19/8~~/18	19-8-18		1/1 L.F.A. moved from Ecoivres to Cambligneul & took over site vacated by 1/2 Highland Field Ambce	
			Visited DDMS & attended conference concerning alterations in Med. Arrangements whereby a Corps. M.D.S. is to be formed, Divisional M.D.S. being abolished as such.	
			S.R. 182 issued regarding move of Division to new area.	
	20-8-18		Corps Med Arrangements No 10 received and issued with SR 181	
			Visited 1/1 and 1/3 L.F. Ambces.	
	21-8-18		1/2nd L.F.A. with 157 Bde moved from Gauchin Legal & now located in the "Y" hutments (Army Map B 1/40000) L 2 c 25. 157 Bde located in close vicinity.	
			1/1 L.F.A. moved to 156 Bde area (– Walrus – Wanquetin – Bernaville – Lattre St. Quentin area) and located at J 23 d 9.1. (~~Army~~ Map 51 c)	
			155 Bde moved to Hermaville – Habarcq – Gouves – Montenescourt area. Sick from this Bde to be collected by 1/2 L.F.A.	
			D.H.Q. closed at 8 am at Villers Chatel and moved to Hermaville, opening at same hour.	
			1/3 L.F.A. stands fast.	

D. D. & L., London, E.C.
(A8504) Wt W1771/M2031 750,000 5/17 Sch. 52 Forms/C2118/14

Army Form C. 2118.

Instructions regarding War Diaries and Intelligence Summaries are contained in F. S. Regs., Part II. and the Staff Manual respectively. Title pages will be prepared in manuscript.

WAR DIARY
~~or~~
~~INTELLIGENCE SUMMARY.~~
(Erase heading not required.)

6

Place	Date	Hour	Summary of Events and Information	Remarks and references to Appendices
Hermaville	~~21~~ 22		RAMC O.O. no 9 issued	
			O.C. 1/1 L.F.A. ordered to send 2 Offrs & 72 bearers to report to O.C. 2/5 N. Mid F.A.	
Bretencourt	23		D.H.Q. closed at Hermaville & opened at Bretencourt at 3pm	
			Conference held in reference to attack by VI Corps.	
			56 Bearers from 1/2 L.F.A. ordered to report for duty with Royal Artillery in the line.	
	~~24~~		1/1 & 1/2 L.F.A. moved to Bretencourt, 1/3 L.F.A. moved to Barly.	
			1/56 Inf Bde attached, passing through 59th Divn holding the line	
			Evacuation of casualties carried by 2/3 N. Mid F.A., supplemented by personnel & equipment from 1/1 & 1/2 L.F.A.	
			1/2 L.F.A. relieved 2/3 N. Mid F. Amb at M.D.S. at R.15.b.6, A.D.S. at M.31.b, & W.W.C.P. at R.29.d	
			1/1 L.F.A. ~~will~~ relieved 2/1 N. Mid F. Amb at Le Fresnoy & Divl Sick Collecting Station	
			1/3 L.F.A. relieved 2/2 N. Mid F. Amb at present running the VI Corps Rest Station. See O.O. no 10	Appendix 2

D. D. & L., London, E.C. (A8:04) Wt W1771/M2031 750,000 5/17 Sch. 52 Forms/C2118/14

Instructions regarding War Diaries and Intelligence Summaries are contained in F. S. Regs., Part II. and the Staff Manual respectively. Title pages will be prepared in manuscript.

WAR DIARY
or
~~INTELLIGENCE SUMMARY.~~

(Erase heading not required.)

Army Form C. 2118.

7

Place	Date	Hour	Summary of Events and Information	Remarks and references to Appendices
Blainville	24		D.H.Q moved to Blainville at 8 am. RAMC O.O. No 11 issued. 1/1 L.F.A. now assisting 1/2 L.F.A. to evacuate front line. 3rd L.F.A. moved from Gouy to Fremont, the Corps Rest Station being handed over to 57 Division 1/1 L.F.A. moved their HQ to M31 b28 & shared that station with 1/2 L.F.A.; an A.D.S was sent forward by the former unit at Mercatel M35a 28. 1/2 L.F.A. now in M31 b28 with A.D.S at S4c. DDMS XVII Corps called	
	25		Visited A.D.S. & found evacuation proceeding well - there being only a few cases to pass through. During night some difficulty in clearing A.D.S at S4c on account of a bridge at S11c86 becoming damaged - this was only a ~~temporary~~ stoppage. 1/2 L.F.A. ~~now~~ moved HQ to S11c & ADS pushed forward	Appendix III RAMC OO No 12

D. D. & L., London, E.C. (A8004) Wt W2771/M2031 750,000 5/17 Sch. 52 Forms/C2118/14

Instructions regarding War Diaries and Intelligence Summaries are contained in F. S. Regs., Part II. and the Staff Manual respectively. Title pages will be prepared in manuscript.

WAR DIARY ~~or~~ INTELLIGENCE ~~SUMMARY.~~

(*Erase heading not required.*)

Army Form C. 2118.

8

Place	Date	Hour	Summary of Events and Information	Remarks and references to Appendices
Blanville			to T1d to keep in touch with the infantry who had advanced during the day.	
			This Division has now been transferred to XVII Corps.	
			Casualties passed through ambces till present number over 1000.	
			Tent subdivision & 8 bearers from 1/3 L.F.A. sent to Corps M.D.S. also 1 M.O. & 4 nursing orderlies sent to C.C.S. under instructions from D.D.M.S.	
	26.8.18		HQrs 1/2 L.F.A. moved forward to S6d91 and A.D.S. to T3a5330 so as to keep in touch with infantry who have today occupied part of the Hindenburg Line. Number of casualties passed through number approx 100.	
			1/3 L.F.A. moved from Fermont to M31b and later to M35a. 1/1 L.F.A. moved HdQrs to M35a, and A.D.S. pushed forward to vicinity of Henin.	
			Visited all Ambce sites & found evacuation progressing well & generally quiet. D.D.M.S. visited M31b28.	

D. D. & L., London, E.C. (A8004) Wt W1771/M2031 750,000 5/17 Sch. 52 Forms/C2118/14

Instructions regarding War Diaries and Intelligence Summaries are contained in F. S. Regs., Part II. and the Staff Manual respectively. Title pages will be prepared in manuscript.

WAR DIARY

~~or~~

~~INTELLIGENCE SUMMARY.~~

(*Erase heading not required.*)

Army Form C. 2118.

9

Place	Date	Hour	Summary of Events and Information	Remarks and references to Appendices
	27		Division was relieved during the night by ~~59th~~ 57th Divn 1/2 & 1/3 L. F. Ambces withdrawn and located in Mercatel area, 1/1 L F A remains in that area. Before withdrawing, all casualties had been cleared from the field of operations. 1/2 L F A had pushed their ADS. forward to Fontaine les Croisilles, but as the majority of wounded were behind in the Hindenburgh line, it was thought advisable to withdraw this ADS. to the original position at T5d	Appendix A RAMC OO No. 13
	28		Division still resting and each ambce located with its respective Brigade. Two Tent subdivisions sent to reinforce 45 and 46 C.C.S by order of D.D.M.S	
	29		O.C. 1/3 L. F. A. ordered to form a CMDS at T2c55, to be prepared to receive ~~patients~~ as soon as completed. ~~Visited~~ all three Ambces	

(A8004) Wt W1771/M2031 750,000 5/17 Sch. 52 Forms/C2118/14 D. D. & L., London, E.C.

Army Form C. 2118.

Instructions regarding War Diaries and Intelligence Summaries are contained in F. S. Regs., Part II. and the Staff Manual respectively. Title pages will be prepared in manuscript.

WAR DIARY

~~or~~

~~INTELLIGENCE SUMMARY.~~

(Erase heading not required.)

10

Place	Date	Hour	Summary of Events and Information	Remarks and references to Appendices
	30		1/3 L. F.A. opened as CMDS. at 0900 ~~today~~.	
			Other Med units remain in their respective Bde. locations	
			OC 1/2 L.F.A. reconnoitring area evacuated by 2/3 London F. Amb	
			56th Division.	
			Orders received to the effect that 52nd Divn will relieve 56th	
			Division in the line on 31st, 1st and 1st-2nd Sept.	
			RAMC O.Order No 14 issued	appendix 5
	31		ADMS Office closed at Blairville and opened at T16C11 at 6pm.	
			2nd L.F.A. relieved 2/3 London F. Ambce in the line with ADS at T23a57	
			relief completed by midnight.	

D. D. & L., London, E.C. (A8004) Wt W1771/M2031 750,000 5/17 Sch. 52 Forms/C2118/14

SECRET. Appendix 1 Sheet 4

Copy No.

R. A. M. C. OPERATION ORDER No. 8
by
COLONEL A. J. MACDOUGALL, A.M.S.
A.D.M.S., 52nd (LOWLAND) DIVISION.
****

15th August, 1918.

Reference - Army Map "B".

I. 1/1st Lowland Fld. Amb. will remain in its present location till the 155th Inf. Bde. moves, when it will take over the quarters vacated by the 1/2nd Highland Field Ambce at CAMBLIGNEUL, W.14, and will collect sick from 155th Inf. Bde. in its new area, GAUCHIN LEGAL.

This unit will evacuate sick of Divisional Artillery in ACQ-FREVIN CAPELLE Area from 16th - 19th instant.

An Advance Party will be sent to-day to hold the quarters to be taken over, under arrangements between Os.C., concerned.

A list of stores taken, and handed over, will be sent to this office.

II 1/2nd Lowland Fld. Amb. will hand over Relay Posts of left and centre Brigades and A. D. S. to 26th Fld. Amb. of 8th Division. Relief to be completed by midnight, 16th/17th instant.

Relay Posts of right Brigade will be handed over to-night (15th) to 1/2nd Highland Fld. Amb., reliefs to be completed by midnight, 15th/16th instant. Main Dressing Station will be handed over to 1/3rd Highland Fld. Amb., relief to be completed by midnight 16th/17th instant.

On relief being completed, 1/2nd Lowland Fld. Amb. will proceed to GOUY SERVINS, Q.35.d. and take over quarters vacated by 1/3rd Highland Fld. Amb. On arrival at new area, 1/2nd Lowland Fld. Amb. will collect sick from 157th Inf. Bde. in the CHATEAU De La HAIE Area.

Details of advance parties to be arranged by Os.C.,concerned.

Attached bearers of 1/1st Lowland Fld. Amb. will be returned to their unit forthwith.

List of stores handed over will be forwarded to this office, differentiating between those handed to the 8th and the 51st Divisions.

III 1/3rd Lowland Fld. Amb., remaining in its present location, will carry on the Divisional Rest Station and will collect sick from the 156th Inf. Bde. when that Brigade moves to the AUBIGNY-SAVY Area ~~from 12th inst. xxxxxxx~~, on 16th instant.

This unit will also arrange to collect sick from 52nd Division Artillery located in ACQ-FREVIN CAPELLE Area from 19th inst.onwards.

IV A.D.M.S. Office will close at MAROEUIL at 9 a.m. on 16th inst. and re-open at VILLERS CHATEL (2 Kilos W. of CAMBLIGNEUL) at the same hour.

ACKNOWLEDGE.

F.W.C. Brown Major
for Colonel, A. M. S.,
A. D. M. S., 52nd (Lowland) Division.

52nd D.H.Q.

Copy No.1 to D.D.M.S.,XVII Corps.
2 A.D.M.S., 8th Divn.
3 A.D.M.S., 51st (Highland) Divn.
4 O.C., 1/1st Low. Fld. Amb.
5 O.C., 1/2nd Low. Fld. Amb.
6 O.C., 1/3rd Low. Fld. Amb.
7 "G", 52nd Divn.

Copy No.8 to "A".
9 "Q"
10 155 Bde.
11 156 Bde.
12 157 Bde.
13 B.G.R.A.
14 No.2?.M.A.C.

Copies 15 & 16 to Diary, No. 17 to FILE.

****

Appendix II Sheet 6

S E C R E T.

Copy No. Diary

R.A.M.C. OPERATION ORDER No. 10
by
COLONEL A.J.MACDOUGALL, A.M.S.,
A.D.M.S., 52nd (LOWLAND) DIVN.

22nd August, 1918.

Reference Maps 51b and 51c.

1. The Field Ambulances of the 52nd Division will relieve the Field Ambulances of the 57th Division.
Relief will be completed by 8.0 ~~a.m.~~ p.m on ~~24th~~ 23rd August, 1918.

2. Relief will be as follows :-
(a) 1/1st Lowland Fld. Amb. will relieve 2/1st North Midland Fld. Amb. at LE FERMONT - R.21.c.8.2./51c. and will take over the Divisional Sick Collecting Station.
O.C., 1/1st L.F.A. will detail one Tent Sub-Division, consisting of 1 Officer and 17 Other Ranks (including 4 clerks already sent) for duty at Corps Main Dressing Station.
All Divisional Cases entered in the Corps Main Dressing Station will be passed through the A. & D. Books of the 1/1st Lowland Fld. Amb. at the Corps Main Dressing Station.
Os.C., 1/2nd & 1/3rd Lowland Fld. Ambs will each send 1 clerk to the Corps Main Dressing Station to relieve two clerks of the 1/1st Lowland Fld. Amb. already there, who will, on relief, return to 1/1st Lowland Fld. Amb.
Ten stretcher bearers of 1/1st Lowland Fld. Amb. have already reported to Corps Main Dressing Station.

(b) 1/2nd Lowland Fld. Amb. will take over from the 2/3rd North Midland Fld. Amb. at L.12.b./51c -
A. D. S. at M.31.b.2.8./51b.
W.W.C.P. at M.32.d.2.9./51c.
and will be responsible for collecting from the Regimental Aid Posts.
One Officer & The Bearers of the 1/1st Lowland Fld. Amb. at present working in the forward area will, during the present situation, remain with the 1/2nd Lowland Fld. Amb. and be available for duty with the latter.

(c) 1/3rd Lowland Fld. Amb. will relieve the 2/2nd North Midland Fld. Amb. at GOUY-en-ARTOIS and will conduct the Corps Rest Station. and Avesnes le Comte

3. Divisional Sick will be sent to the Corps Rest Station for treatment, through other Fld. Ambces. Attention is called to VIth. Corps Medical Arrangements No. XIV, para. 5.

4. D. M. S., Third Army No. 3073/4/65 of 20/8/18 is published for information and necessary action :- "From receipt of this letter until further orders, only serious cases of sickness will be evacuated to C.C.Ss. of this Army"

5. Completion of moves will be reported to this office immediately after taking over.

ACKNOWLEDGE.

[signature] Maj for Colonel, A. M. S.,
A.D.M.S., 52nd (Lowland) Division.

Copy No. 1 to 1/1st L.F.A.; No.2 to 1/2nd L.F.A.; No.3 to 1/3rd L.F.A.
No. 4 to "Q", 52nd Div; No.5 to "G", 52nd Div;
No. 6 to A.D.M.S., 57th Divn.

Appendix 3. Sheet 7

S E C R E T.

Copy No. 5

R.A.M.C. OPERATION ORDER No. 12
by
COLONEL A.J.MACDOUGALL, A.M.S.,
A.D.M.S., 52nd (LOWLAND) DIVN.

25th AUGUST,1918.

Reference Map 51c.

1. 156th Inf. Bde will cross the line of the road NEUVILLE VITASSE - HENIN through 156th Inf. Bde.
156th Bde. H.Q. will be in the sunken road at M.35.d.central.
The general objective of the Division will be towards FONTAINE CROISILLES.

2. Casualties may be expected at about N.21.,22.,27.;and HENIN and MARTIN Trenches may be used for evacuation.
In the latter stages, the neighbourhood of HENIN, as well supplied with roads, may be useful for an A.D.S.

3. O.C., 1/3rd Low. Fld. Amb. will be prepared to move,at short notice, to the old A.D.S. at M.31.b.3.8. and await further orders there.
On arriving there, one officer and bearers of 1/3rd L.F.A. attached to 1/1st L.F.A. will come under orders of their own C.O. who will be prepared to use them independantly or to assist the other Ambulances. Cars of 1/3rd L.F.A. at present attached 1/2nd L.F.A.will come under command of O.C., 1/3rd L.F.A. when the latter has orders to move forward of M.31.b.

4. Owing to a shortage of lorries, empty returning lorries passing the Corps Main Dressing Station will be used where possible under the following conditions - (a) that an orderly, (returning by empty Ambulance Cars from C.M.D.S.) accompanies each lorry, and (b) that the lorry is not delayed.
Ambulance Motor Cars should be reserved, as much as possible, for stretcher cases.

5. Car orderlies will see that splints, blankets and stretchers are replenished from C.M.D.S.

6. Os.C., Field Ambces will indent direct on O.C., C.M.D.S. for dressings urgently required.

7. Os.C., Fld. Ambces are empowered to indent, on the authority of A.D.M.S., 52nd Division, for ambulance cars from C.M.D.S. but this authority will only be used when absolutely necessary, and the cars sent back as soon as the necessity for them has ceased. No of cars indented for will be reported to this office.

8. O.C., 1/2nd L.F.A. will send one lorry to O.C., 1/1st L.F.A. and retain one himself.
Horsed Ambulances should be used in the early stages of the operations to supplement lorries as far as A.D.S., M.31.b.

9. Divisional H.Q. will be at the Quarries, BLAIRVILLE.

O.C., 1/2nd L.F.A., if in urgent need of Ambulance Cars, should apply to O.C., 1/3rd L.F.A. who will assist with cars if the situation on the left flank permits.

ACKNOWLEDGE.

Issued at 2345

A.J. MacDougall
Colonel, A.M.S.,
A.D.M.S., 52nd (Lowland) Division.

Copy No.1 to 1st L.F.A.
2 2nd L.F.A. No. 5 & 6 to Diary.
3 3rd L.F.A. 7 FILE.

Appendix 4 Sheet 9 Diary.

R.A.M.C. OPERATION ORDER No.13. COPY No. 4
by
COLONEL A.J.MACDOUGALL, A.M.S.,
A.D.M.S., 52nd.(Lowland) Divn.

Reference Map 51 B S.W. (Herewith) 27th. August, 1918.

1. Information.
156th. Inf. Bde. will attack under barrage coming down on line N.36.c.5.7. and N.30.d.5.2. at 1000 hrs. and move forward with Right on FONTAINE CROISILLES. 155 Inf. Bde. will clear Hindenburg Front and Support Lines as far as FOOLEY LANE at all costs by 0900, mop up Hindenburg Line in rear of 157th. Inf. Bde., when they will re-organise at once and come into Divisional Reserve on HENIN HILL. 157th. Inf. Bde. will attack at 0920 to take FONTAINE CROISILLES. Barrages remain on general line E. of FONTAINE CROISILLES for 30 minutes. When they lift, Brigades push on - 156th. Bde. for HENDECOURT and 157th. Bde. for RIENCOURT.

2. MEDICAL ARRANGEMENTS.
O.C. 3rd. L.F.A. will establish an Adv. Dressing Statn. in the Hindenburg Line as soon as the line has been cleared.
Os.C. 1st. and 2nd. L.F.As. will keep in touch with their respective Brigades and will form Adv. Drsg. Stns. to conform with the situation.
Positions of A.D.Ss. should be reported to this office as soon as established.

3. ACKNOWLEDGE.

Issued at 0630

Colonel, A.M.S.,
27/8/18. A.D.M.S., 52nd.(Lowland) Division.

A.D.M.S.,
52nd DIVISION.
No. 1K198
Date.

Copy No.1 to 1st. L.F.A.
2 2nd. L.F.A.
3 3rd. L.F.A.
4 Diary
5 -"-
6 File.

Appendix 5 Sheet 10

S E C R E T. Copy No. 5

R.A.M.C. OPERATION ORDER No. 14
by
A.D.M.S., 52nd (LOWLAND) DIVISION.
==========================

30th August, 1918.

1. (a) 155th Inf. Bde will relieve 169th Inf. Bde. 56th Division, on HENIN HILL to-morrow, 31st instant, (H.Q., T.4.b.8.8.). Relief to be completed by 1300.

(b) 155th Inf. Bde will move from HENIN HILL and relieve 168th Inf. Bde. 56th Division, (H.Q., U.7.d.7.7.) in BULLECOURT Battle Line, relief to be completed by 0400, 1st Septr.

(c) 156th Inf. Bde will move to-morrow, 31st instant, from bivouac area and relieve 167th Inf. Bde. 56th Division (H.Q., U.7.c.98.80.), in Support to Battle Line; Brigade not to pass E. of the high ground T.10.b.3 d., T.14.a., before 2003.

(d) 157th Inf. Bde. to move to HENIN HILL area on 1st Septr., (H.Q., T.4.b.8.8.) to arrive by 1000.

During night 31st/1st, 157th Inf. Bde. will be ready to move at one hour's notice.

2. Following moves of Field Ambulances will take place -

(a) 1/2nd Lowland Fld. Amb. will relieve the 2/3rd London Fld. Amb. at the A.D.S., T.22.b.8.6.(time of relief to be notified later) with one Tent Sub-Division. The Ambulance, less Tent Sub-Division for A.D.S. will park in the vicinity of T.14.a. Two bearer sub-divisions under an officer will be held in readiness to act with 157th Inf. Bde. O.C., Bearers will report to 157th Bde. H.Q. before 1800 on 31st instant. O.C., Fld. Amb. will be prepared to advance his A.D.S. when necessary, and will report change of A.D.S. to the nearest Bde.H.Q. and to this office.

(b) 1/1st Lowland Fld. Amb. will move to the neighbourhood of the Corps Main Dressing Station, T.1.c.5.5. and will park its transport there; move to be completed by 1800 on 31st instant. Two bearer sub-divisions, under an officer, will join 156th Inf. Bde. and will be responsible for the evacuation of wounded to the A.D.S. The officer will report to H.Q., 156th Inf. Bde. before the Brigade leaves the bivouac area to arrange details and ascertain positions of R.A.Ps.

(c) 1/3rd Lowland Fld. Amb. will remain in its present position. O.C., 1/3rd L.F.A. will detail an officer and two bearer sub-divisions for duty with 155th Inf. Bde. who will be responsible for the evacuation of the wounded of the Bde. to the A.D.S. O.C., Bearers will report to 155th Inf. Bde.H.Q. and arrange details of positions of R.A.Ps.

3. OsC., Fld. Ambces will attach one orderly, as runner, to Bde. H.Q. of the Bde with which they are working.

OsC., 1/1st and 1/3rd Low. Fld. Ambs will each put at the disposal of O.C., 1/2nd Low. Fld. Amb. four ambulance cars and two horsed ambulance wagons.

O.C., 1/1st Low. Fld. Amb. will be responsible for collecting sick from the Bdes in the HENIN HILL Area.

4. Headquarters, 52nd Division will close at BLAIRVILLE QUARRY at 1800, 31st instant and re-open at dug-outs, T.21.d. same hour.

Brigade Headquarters, after completion of moves noted in para 1 will be - 155th Inf. Bde. - U.7.d.7.7.; 156th Inf. Bde.- U.7.c.9.8.; 157th Inf. Bde.- T.4.b.8.8.

ACKNOWLEDGE.

Issued at 2345

[signature]
Colonel, A.M.S.,
A.D.M.S., 52nd (Lowland) Division.

Copy No. 1 to 1/1st L.F.A.
2 1/2nd L.F.A.
3 1/3rd L.F.A.
4 A.D.M.S., 56th Divn.

13

Instructions regarding War Diaries and Intelligence Summaries are contained in F. S. Regs., Part II. and the Staff Manual respectively. Title pages will be prepared in manuscript.

WAR DIARY
or
INTELLIGENCE SUMMARY.
(Erase heading not required.)

Army Form C. 2118.

Vol 6

Place	Date	Hour	Summary of Events and Information	Remarks and references to Appendices
Sept 1918			Confidential War Diary of D.D.M.S. 52nd Division. Sept. 1st to Sept. 31st. 1918 VOLUME 9.	140/3323

D. D. & L., London, E.C.
A6001 Wt. 1 71/M2031 750,000 5/17 Sch. 52 Forms C2118/14

Instructions regarding War Diaries and Intelligence Summaries are contained in F. S. Regs., Part II. and the Staff Manual respectively. Title pages will be prepared in manuscript.

WAR DIARY
or
~~INTELLIGENCE SUMMARY.~~
(Erase heading not required.)

Army Form C. 2118.

Sheet 1

Place	Date	Hour	Summary of Events and Information	Remarks and references to Appendices
Map 51B SW	1 Sept	9am	ADMS Office T16 c11. 1/2 L.F.A. forming A.D.S. at T23 a 5.7.	
			1/1 L.F.A. moved to T14 b 51 & held in reserve	
			1/3 L.F.A. acting as Corps Main Dressing Station at T1 c 5.5	
		~~Noon~~	R.A.M.C. Operation Order No 15 issued	Appendix I.
		3am.	ADS 2 L.F.A. moved to U 20 d 94	
	2 Sept	9am	Division advancing. A.D.S. not yet moved owing to bad condition of roads but Car collecting posts pushed forward to U 21 d 1.2.	
		11am	Horsed ambce & Car posts now established at U22 c43 and U27 d26. Roads forward of these points impassible for vehicles	
		7.30pm	Ambce wagon post at C4 b52; cases transferred to Ambce Cars at U27 d26. Cases passed through A.D.S. for past 24 hours number 240	
			1/1 L.F.A. moved up as reserve to T22 b 28	

(A8c04) D. D. & L., London, E.C. Wt W1771/M2031 750,000 5/17 Sch. 52 Forms/C2118/14

Army Form C. 2118.

Instructions regarding War Diaries and Intelligence Summaries are contained in F. S. Regs., Part II. and the Staff Manual respectively. Title pages will be prepared in manuscript.

WAR DIARY
~~or~~
~~INTELLIGENCE SUMMARY.~~
(Erase heading not required.)

Sheet 2

Place	Date	Hour	Summary of Events and Information	Remarks and references to Appendices
	3rd	2.25	RAMC Operation Wire 545 issued. 155 Bde & 157 Bde attacking at 5am.	
		8.30	A.D.S. now moved forward to Queant – C12 b5.9	
		10.30am	1/1 L.F.A. moved to U20d & ordered to hold party in readiness to form A.D.S. forward of that point.	
		9/pm	Warning ordered issued to effect that Division now in Corps support	
	4th		Location of F. Ambces as yesterday, but Car post pushed out to D9 b2.2. Visited A.D.S. 1/2 L.F.A.	
	5th	8am	HeadQrs ~~& transport~~ of 1/2 L.F.A. moved to Morcourt owing to shelling during night which caused 4 casualties to personnel and 14 to animals. Operation Order No. 15 issued.	
	6th		Division today withdrawn and concentrated in St. Ledger area. 1/1 L.F.A. moved to B3 b50 and attending sick	

D. D. & L., London, E.C. (A8004) Wt W1771/M2031 750,000 5/17 Sch. 52 Forms/C2118/14

Instructions regarding War Diaries and Intelligence Summaries are contained in F. S. Regs., Part II. and the Staff Manual respectively. Title pages will be prepared in manuscript.

WAR DIARY
or
~~INTELLIGENCE SUMMARY.~~
(*Erase heading not required.*)

Army Form C. 2118.

Sheet 3

Place	Date	Hour	Summary of Events and Information	Remarks and references to Appendices
			of the 156 Bde. 1/2 L.F.A. moved to U25 a 2.0. and attending sick of 155 and 157 Bdes.	
	7/9/18		Visited M.D.S.	
	8/9/18		Division still resting. Weather broken down & boisterous, rendering the adoption of Sanitary measures very difficult.	
	9/9/18		OC 1/2 L.F.A. ordered to reconnoitre the forward area, in view of the possibility of this Division taking over the line.	
	10/9/18		Examined men of 155 Bde at 1/2 L.F.A. for reclassification purposes. Warning Order to the effect that this Division would probably relieve 56 Div on 16th inst.	
	11/9/18		Inspected units of 155 Bde. Med. arrangements in event of an advance being forward sent to 'G' office for information.	
	12/9/18		Examined men of 156 Bde for reclassification purposes at 1/1 L.F.A.	

D. D. & L., London, E.C.
(A8co4) Wt W1771/M2031 750,000 5/17 Sch. 52 Forms/C2118/14

Instructions regarding War Diaries and Intelligence Summaries are contained in F. S. Regs., Part II. and the Staff Manual respectively. Title pages will be prepared in manuscript.

WAR DIARY

~~or~~

~~INTELLIGENCE SUMMARY.~~

(Erase heading not required.)

Army Form C. 2118.

Sheet 4

Place	Date	Hour	Summary of Events and Information	Remarks and references to Appendices
	13/9/18		Visited A.D.M.S at Queant to make arrangements for relief of his units.	
	14/9/18		Units of 156 Inf Bde inspected as regards sanitation. Up till now only improvised box latrines & open deep trenches have been available. Application to the San Sectn has borne no fruit.	
			52nd Divn OO 131 Received. 52nd Divn will relieve 57th Divn in the line on 17/16 and 16/17th inst.	
	15/9/18		O.O. No 17 issued.	Appendix III
	16/9/18		1/1 L.F.A. took over ADS & forward posts from 2/2 Wessex F.A. relief complete at 2pm.	
Queant	17/9/18		1/2 L.F.A. moved to C9 central, to be held in reserve & ready to join the Advanced Guard if formed.	
			Divl Headquarters moved to Queant today at 10 am.	
	18/9/18		Warning order from "G" Branch received, to the effect that Canadian Corps would take over left sector of the present Divl	

D. D. & L., London, E.C. (A8001) Wt W1771/M2031 750,000 5/17 Sch. 52 Forms/C2118/14

Instructions regarding War Diaries and Intelligence Summaries are contained in F. S. Regs., Part II. and the Staff Manual respectively. Title pages will be prepared in manuscript.

WAR DIARY
or
~~INTELLIGENCE SUMMARY.~~
(Erase heading not required.)

Army Form C. 2118.

Sheet 5.

Place	Date	Hour	Summary of Events and Information	Remarks and references to Appendices
			Area on night 19/20 inst. Capt Ross attd 1/5 H.L.I. died from wounds in 1/1 L.F.A. last night.	
	19.9.18		Warning order received to the effect that 157 Bde would be relieved in the L. Sector of present Divl front on night 19/20 by 2nd Canadian Divn. This order was confirmed later. The present A.D.S. in Inchy will remain under administration of this Office but a "holding party" will be sent by Canadian F. Amb. in case of this Dressing Station being given up on short notice.	
	do		Visited ADMS Guards Divn with a view to becoming acquainted with the med arrangements of that Division, which is at present on our R. flank.	
		5 pm	52 Divl O.O. No 100 received to the effect that 155 will recapture Moeuvres tonight, the attack commencing at 7 pm. In consequence a further subdivision of bearers (& officer) was ordered to report to the Brigade Bearer Officer.	

D. D. & L., London, E.C. (A8004) Wt W1771/M2031 750,000 5/17 Sch. 52 Forms/C2118/14

Instructions regarding War Diaries and Intelligence Summaries are contained in F. S. Regs., Part II. and the Staff Manual respectively. Title pages will be prepared in manuscript.

WAR DIARY
or
~~INTELLIGENCE SUMMARY.~~
(Erase heading not required.)

Army Form C. 2118.

Sheet 6

Place	Date	Hour	Summary of Events and Information	Remarks and references to Appendices
	20/9/18		Moeuvres Operation successful – casualties approx 150. 157 Bde moved from line to Noreuil area. 156 Bde moved to Queant - Pronville area in support of 155 Bde holding (Moeuvres) sector of front line. Corps line only consists of 1 Bde front now.	
	21/9/18		Orders received from G.S. to effect ~~that~~ this Div would take over part of line held at present by the L. Bde of the Division on our immediate right. For this purpose one Battn of 157 Bde will hold this line and will be under command of G.O.C. [illegible]. Evacuation from this Battn will be done by hand carry [illegible] existing posts used by 156 Bde units. Extra bearers [illegible] Bearer Officer 1/2 156 Bde to assist.	
	22/9/18		Situation quiet.	
	23/9/18		155 Bde relieved 156 Bde in the line ~~tonight~~. Evacuations running through present posts.	

D. D. & L., London, E.C. (A8004) Wt W1771/M2031 750,000 5/17 Sch. 52 Forms/C2118/14

Instructions regarding War Diaries and Intelligence Summaries are contained in F. S. Regs., Part II. and the Staff Manual respectively. Title pages will be prepared in manuscript.

WAR DIARY
~~or~~
~~INTELLIGENCE SUMMARY.~~
(*Erase heading not required.*)

Army Form C. 2118.

Sheet 7

Place	Date	Hour	Summary of Events and Information	Remarks and references to Appendices
	24/9/18		52 Div G. Order No 108 received, re attack of 17 Corps in conjunction of Canadian & VI Corps on the flanks	
	25/9/18		RAMC Operation Order 8 issued. Appendix	III
			Notification received from 2nd Canadn Divn to the effect that the A.D.S. in Queant would be required by them on 26th Queant is outside this Divl boundary.	
	26/9/18		1/2 L.F.A. moved & occupied new site on main Bapaume Cambrai Road 1/2 L.F.A. moved from Queant to S. of Pronville. Two lines of evacuation are possible One via relay posts in Hindenburg Line to Pronville, the other via main Bapaume Cambrai Road to ADS of 2 L.F.A. Cars have been pushed as far forward as possible	
	27/9/18		Cases nearly all coming through relay posts in Hindenburg Line and tending to cause an accumulation at ADS, Pronville	

D. D. & L., London, E.C. (A8co4) Wt W1771/M2031 750,000 5/17 Sch. 52 Forms/C2118/14

Instructions regarding War Diaries and Intelligence Summaries are contained in F. S. Regs., Part II. and the Staff Manual respectively. Title pages will be prepared in manuscript.

WAR DIARY
or
INTELLIGENCE SUMMARY.
(*Erase heading not required.*)

Army Form C. 2118.

Sheet 8.

Place	Date	Hour	Summary of Events and Information	Remarks and references to Appendices
			This is almost entirely due to a large majority of the cases being men of 63rd Division. Road intended for evacuating to M.D.S. has been blocked by heavy guns, & traffic on remaining road renders this route a very slow method of evacuation as Motor Ambces can go at only a horse walking pace.	
		10.30	MAC wired for extra transport. DDMS also phoned re this.	
		2pm	No extra transport yet arrived; cases now number approx 200 — chiefly men of 63rd Divn. ADMS 63 Divn phoned for assistance. All spare Ambulances sent to this A.D.S. Forward Bearer Officers told to discontinue evacuating to Proville & to use 2 LFA ADS at ~~[illegible]~~ J9b.	
		6pm.	Some assistance now from 63rd Divn and MAC. Cases being got away gradually.	

D. D. & L., London, E.C. (A5003) Wt. W1771/M2031 750,000 5/17 Sch. 52 Forms C2118/14

Instructions regarding War Diaries and Intelligence Summaries are contained in F. S. Regs., Part II. and the Staff Manual respectively. Title pages will be prepared in manuscript.

WAR DIARY
or
~~INTELLIGENCE SUMMARY.~~
(Erase heading not required.)

Army Form C. 2118.

Sheet 9.

Place	Date	Hour	Summary of Events and Information	Remarks and references to Appendices
			ADS at J 9 b not had many cases to deal with – approx in all 150 cases. Two Motor Ambces were put out of action on this route of evacuation this morning.	
		11.30 pm	In ADS Pronville there remain 40 British & 40 Germans to be evacuated – all stretcher cases. Left now total number of cases passing through must approx be 1000 – (200 of which were Germans & 423 men of 63rd Div)	
	29/9/18	1.30 am	All British evacuated now	
		8.30	All Germans now evacuated. No fresh cases arriving.	
			½ L.F.A moved from Pronville and now located D29 c 85, 00 as to be near main Cambrai-Bapaume road.	
			⅓ L.F.A occupied in closing down CMDS at U25 central & moving to vicinity of new CMDS at J9 b.	
			Received orders from "G" Branch to effect that 155 Bde would	

D. D. & L., London, E.C.
(A8001) Wt. W1771/M2031 750,000 5/17 Sch. 52 Forms C2118/14

Army Form C. 2118.

WAR DIARY
or
~~INTELLIGENCE SUMMARY.~~
(Erase heading not required.)

Instructions regarding War Diaries and Intelligence Summaries are contained in F. S. Regs., Part II. and the Staff Manual respectively. Title pages will be prepared in manuscript.

Sheet 10

Place	Date	Hour	Summary of Events and Information	Remarks and references to Appendices
			move to Amiens Grandcourt area tomorrow 30th	
			Arranged for two motor Ambces to be sent to Bearer officer at new Bde H.Q.rs for evacuation of sick to 2/1th in vicinity of CMDS	
			DDMS telephoned to say that he wished OC 2/1th to be prepared to open new CMDS in vicinity of F20 c	
			This has been communicated to that unit.	
			Division resting & no great number of cases being evacuated.	
			On instruction recd from DDMS, 5 motor Ambces sent to 15th MAC.	
	30/9		Orders received that this Divn would relieve 63rd Divn in the line on night 1/2 Oct.	
			RAMC Op. Order No 19 issued. Appendix IV.	
			[signature] Major for ADMS 52 Div	
	1/10		1/1 L FA now located F28 c 65 complete & in reserve.	
			1/2 L FA took over forward area and pushed ADS forward to F28 d 49 & withdrew car post a few hundred yards from bridge over canal	

D. D. & L., London, E.C. A(00) Wt. 1 71/M2031 750,000 5/17 Sch. 52 Forms C2118/14

Appendix I. Sheet I.

S E C R E T. Copy No. 7

R.A.M.C. OPERATION ORDER No. 16
by
A.D.M.S., 52nd (LOWLAND) DIVISION.

oooooooooooooooooooooooo

1st September, 1918.

1. (a) 156th Inf. Bde. will pass through 155th Inf. Bde. and clear area MOULIN SANS SOUCI - the road in U.30.b. as far as cross roads in V.25.c.6.2. - D.1.a.3.1. - C.[illegible].b.9.0.

(b) 155th Inf. Bde. will move up their right to keep touch between the 3rd Division on their extreme right and the right of the attack of the 156th Inf. Bde.

(c) 155th Inf. Bde. will then attack through 156th Inf. Bde. and mop up HINDENBURG LINE as far S. as QUEANT - LAGNICOURT Road.

(d) 157th Inf. Bde. will be prepared to move up and push through 156th Inf. Bde. and mop up HINDENBURG Support Line as far as communication trench V.30.d.1.9. to V.29.d.1.4.

(e) 157th Inf. Bde. will ~~be prepared to~~ move at 8 a.m. on 2nd instant to area U.13.b. - U.7.d. and await orders from Division.

2. (a) On the 157th Inf. Bde. leaving HENIN HILL Area, O.C., 1/1st Low. Fld. Amb. will withdraw Car Post at N.35.d.3.9. and the car will rejoin ambulance at 6 a.m., 2nd instant. He will hold a tent sub-division with equipment ready to move and form a dressing station at half an hour's notice.

(b) O.C., 1/2nd Low. Fld. Amb. will be responsible that two sub-divisions of his bearers join the 157th Inf. Bde. in area U.13.b. -U.7.d. at 8 a.m. on 2nd instant, if not already posted. He will hold in readiness a Tent sub-division to form an A.D.S. in the neighbourhood of BULLECOURT as soon as the situation permits and will inform this office immediately of its location.

As soon as 157th Inf. Bde. advances from area U.13.b. and U.7.d. the car post at U.7. will be withdrawn.

3. ZERO hour will be notified later.

4. ACKNOWLEDGE.

[signature]
Colonel, A.M.S.,
A.D.M.S., 52nd (Lowland) Division.

Issued at 1930.

Copy No. 1. to 1/1st L.F.A.
2 1/2nd L.F.A.
3 "Q"
4 A.D.M.S., 57th Divn.
5 A.D.M.S., 3rd Division.
6 Diary.
7 Diary.
8 File.

oooooooooooooooooooo

Appendix II
Sheet 4.

SECRET. Copy No. 9

R.A.M.C. OPERATION ORDER No. 17
BY
A.D.M.S., 52nd (Lowland) Division.
****

14th September, 1918.

1. INFORMATION. 52nd Division (less Artillery) will relieve 57th Division (less Artillery) in front line of the XVII Corps Sector on nights 15th/16th and 16th/17th September.

155th Inf. Bde. will take over the Right Section on night 15th/16th. During 15th inst. 155th Inf. Bde. will concentrate in the HIRONDELLE Valley, S.W. of QUEANT and will not pass Eastward of a N. and S. line drawn through West edge of QUEANT before 8 p.m.

156th Bde. will relieve the Support Bde. of 57th Division by daylight on 16th instant.

157th Bde. will relieve Left Bde. Section on night of 16th/17th under same arrangements, as regards time, as 155th Bde.

2. MEDICAL ARRANGEMENTS.

(a) Locations of Medical Posts.
Car Collecting Posts :- D.6.d.6.1. and D.9.d.5.2.
Trolley Post. :- D.11.d.5.0.
Wheeler Posts. :- D.18.b.4.1.and D.12.b.6.0.
Advanced Dressing Station. :- D.1.d.6.8.
Corps Main Dressing Station:- U.25.central.

(b) O.C., 1/1st Low. Fld. Amb. will take over the A.D.S. and Posts from 2/2nd Wessex Fld. Amb. and will be responsible for the evacuation from the Collecting Posts and to the Corps Main Dressing Station. Relief to be completed by 2 p.m.15th inst. Details of relief to be arranged between Ambulance Commanders concerned.

(c) Os.C., 1/2nd and 1/3rd Low. Fld. Ambs will each attach one Bearer Sub-Division, under an Officer, to their respective Bdes. All details will be arranged between Bearer Officers and Bde. H.Q. concerned. The remaining Bearers of these Fld. Ambs will be held in reserve.

(d) O.C., 1/2nd Low. Fld. Amb. will move to a site at C.11.c.7.6. and hold his Ambulance (less the above-mentioned Bearer Sub-Division) in reserve - move to be completed by 8 p.m. on 16th instant.

(e) O.C., 1/3rd Low. Fld. Amb. will continue to conduct the Corps Main Dressing Station.

3. GENERAL. Each bearer will be in possession of a stretcher sling which should be marked with his name and number and should always be in his possession.

All ranks will salve abandoned stretchers and return them to the A.D.S. in order to prevent a shortage of stretchers.

O.C., Bearers will see that stretchers sent from R.A.Ps are promptly replaced.

All Field Medical Cards will be signed in full - not merely initialled - by the Medical Officer concerned.

4. Owing to the danger of gas during relief, the greatest care will be taken throughout the relief to conceal any extra movement by daylight, especially on the high ground between NOREUIL and ECOUST, and on that immediately W. of QUEANT.

Sections of Fld. Ambs. will march at 100 yards intervals. The same distance will be maintained between every four vehicles of any description. Closing up must be specially guarded against.

5./

5. Locations of Brigade Headquarters, after taking over, will be as follows :-

155th Inf. Bde. H. Q. - - - - D.15.b.5.6.
156th Inf. Bde. H. Q. - - - - C.3.b.4.8.
157th Inf. Bde. H. Q. - - - - V.28.d.0.0.

Position of Divisional Headquarters will be wired to all concerned as soon as possible.

6. Completion of moves will be reported by Os.C., 1/1st and 1/2nd Low. Fld. Ambs to this office. O.C., 1/1st Low. Fld. Amb. will also include a list of stores taken over.

7. ACKNOWLEDGE. (Field Ambulances only.)

A.J. MacDougall
Colonel, A. M. S.,
A. D. M. S., 52nd (Lowland) Division.

Issued at 11 pm......

=*=*=*=*=*=*=*=*=*=*=*=

Copy No. 1 to 1/1st L. F. A.
2 1/2nd L. F. A.
3 1/3rd L. F. A.
4 H.Q., 52nd Divn.
5 155th Inf. Bde.
6 156th Inf. Bde.
7 157th Inf. Bde.
8 A.D.M.S., 57th Divn.
9 ✓ Diary.
10 Diary.
11 File.

=================

Appendix I
Sheet

S E C R E T.

Copy No. 26

R.A.M.C. OPERATION ORDER No. 18
by
A.D.M.S., 52nd (Lowland) DIVISION.
****

25th Sept.,1918.

Reference - Map 57c.N.E.,1/20,000.and 52nd Divn.Order No.136.

1. 52nd Division will carry out operations at a date to be noted later.
The 63rd Division will be on the Left, the Guards Division on the Right.

2. (a) O.C., 1/1st Low. Fld. Amb. will be in charge of present A.D.S. at D.1.d.5.9. and present Car Posts.
He will send one Motor Lorry for walking wounded to O.C., 1/2nd Low. Fld. Amb. on demand.
He will be responsible for the evacuation of 156th Inf. Bde.

(b) O.C., 1/2nd Low. Fld. Amb. will form an A.D.S. at J.9.b.4.1. and a Car Post at J.12.a.2.7. at ZERO Hour.
He will hold a Tent Sub-Division in readiness to form a further A.D.S. and Car Posts as the situation demands, reporting sites to this office and Bearer Officers.
He will be responsible for evacuation of wounded from 157th Bde. and from 52nd Bn. M.G.C. (R.A.P.- E.25.b.7.3.)

(c) O.C., 1/3rd Low. Fld. Amb. will conduct the Corps Main Dressing Station and will be responsible, through his Bearer Officer,for evacuation of 155th Bde. He will, on demand, place two ambulance motor cars at the disposal of O.C., 1/1st Low. Fld. Amb. and two at the disposal of O.C., 1/2nd Low. Fld. Amb. He will also place three horsed ambulance wagons and three riding horses at the disposal of O.C.,1/2nd Low. Fld. Amb.

3. Attention is called to my No. M.O./361 of 21/9/18, "Evacuation of Wounded", forwarded to Fld. Ambulances, all Medical Officers and Brigade Headquarters. These instructions will be strictly complied with.

4. O.C., A.D.S. will be responsible that all Car Posts are marked by a flag or notice board, and O.C., Bearers, that the route for Bearers is indicated by directing posts. When a route is abandoned, these will be withdrawn.

5. (a) Horsed Ambulance Wagons and wheeled stretchers will be used wherever possible.
(b) All ranks will salve abandoned stretchers and blankets and return them to the nearest Relay Post in order to prevent a shortage of stretchers.
(c) OsC.,A.D.S., Os.i/c,Bearers, and M.Os., on being relieved by a Unit not belonging to this Division, will obtain a receipt for all blankets, stretchers etc. handed over as area stores and will send a list of such to this office.
(d) Field Medical Cards will be signed in full, not merely initialled, by the M.O. concerned, and will be made out at the A.D.S.
(e) Morphia will be given hypodermically - not by the mouth. The dose, and hour at which given, must be entered on the Field Medical Card
(f) The advantage of hot drinks, with bicarbonate of soda, in haemorrhage shock must be remembered.

6./

6. As directed in my No. M.O./361, Os.C., Fld. Ambs and A.D.Ss will forward reports sent by Os.C., Bearers, first reading the report and taking action if necessary, reporting to this office when forwarding the reports what action has been taken.

Os.C., Field Ambulances will render a situation report to this office at 5 a.m. and 5 p.m.

Attention of Field Ambulance Commanders is called to Corps Medical Arrangements already circulated to them.

7. LOCATIONS.

A.D.M.S. Office ---------------------------- D.7.a.5.7.
Left A.D.S. -- D.1.d.5.9. closes at 9 a.m. on 26/9/18,
opens 9 a.m. on 26/9/18 at D.15.b.5.5.
Car Post ----------------------------------- D.15.d.5.5.
Horsed Ambulance Post.---------------------- D.17.b.1.3.
Trolley Post. ------------------------------ D.17.a.5.9.
Relay Posts ---------------------------------D.17.d.1.8.
D.18.c.5.8.
D.18.d.8.6.
E.19.a.0.9.
E.19.a.8.5.
Regimental Aid Posts ----------------------- E.13.d.0.8.
D.18.d.2.3.
E.19.a.8.3.
E.19.a.1.9.

The following open on ZERO Day -
Right A. D. S. ---------------- J.9.b.5.1.
Car Post - Right. ------------- J.12.a.2.7.
Left ------------- D.22.a.9.5.

8. ACKNOWLEDGE. (Fld. Ambs only.)

A.F. MacDougall

Issued at ..1900..hrs.

Colonel, A.M.S.,
A. D. M. S., 52nd (Lowland) Division.

****

Copy No.	To	No.	To
1.	1/1st L. F. A.	15.	M.O.i/c, 1/5th H.L.I.
2.	1/2nd L. F. A.	16.	M.O.i/c, 1/6th H.L.I.
3.	1/3rd L. F. A.	17.	M.O.i/c, 1/7th H.L.I.
4.	"A" & "Q", 52nd Div.	18.	M.O.i/c, 9th Bde.RFA.
5.	"G", 52nd Divn.	19.	M.O.i/c, 56th " "
6.	155th Inf. Bde.	20.	M.O.i/c, 52nd M.G.Bn.
7.	156th Inf. Bde.	21.	M.O.i/c, 17th N. F.
8.	157th Inf. Bde.	22.	A.D.M.S., 63rd Div.
9.	M.O.i/c, 1/4th R.S.F.	23.	A.D.M.S., Guards Div.
10.	M.O.i/c, 1/5th R.S.F.	24.	C.R.A., 52nd Divn.
11.	M.O.i/c, 1/4th K.O.S.B.	25.	D.D.M.S., 17 Corps.
12.	M.O.i/c, 1/4th R.Scots.	26. 27.	Diary.
13.	M.O.i/c, 1/7th R.Scots.		
14.	M.O.i/c, 1/7th S. R.	28.	File.

****

Appendix IV Sheet 10

S E C R E T.

Copy No. 12

R.A.M.C. OPERATION ORDER No. 19
by
A.D.M.S., 52nd (LOWLAND) DIVISION.

1st October, 1918.

1. 155th Inf. Bde. will relieve 63rd (R.N.) Division in the line by midnight, 1st/2nd October, being prepared to push on, on 2nd October, 1918.

157th Inf. Bde. will move at 1400 and occupy MARCOING Line (F.30.) in Divisional Support.

156th Inf. Bde. will move, not before 1600, to L.3.a. and L.3.c. and be in Divisional Reserve.

2. 1/1st Lowland Fld. Amb. will relieve 150th Fld. Amb. today at E.28.a.5.6

1/2nd Lowland Fld. Amb. will relieve 148th Fld. Amb. today at A.D.S., F.25.a.3.7., and Car Posts, F.29.b.4.6. and will be & F.28.d.6.9. responsible for evacuating from the Front Line.

1/3rd Lowland Fld. Amb. will remain in its present site.

3. O.C., 1/2nd Lowland Fld. Amb. will be prepared to form a further A.D.S. when the situation demands and the site at F.25.a.3.7. will be taken over by the 1/1st Low. Fld. Amb. and carried on till the further A.D.S. is open. O.C., 1/2nd Low. Fld. Amb. will inform O.C., 1/1st Low. Fld. Amb. when he is advancing.

4. The following will be placed at the disposal of O.C., 1/2nd Low. Fld. Amb. :-

By O.C., 1/3rd Low. Fld. Amb. - - - 3 horsed ambulance wagons.
2 ambulance motor cars.

By O.C., 1/1st Low. Fld. Amb. - - - 4 ambulance motor cars.

to be used in evacuating A.D.S..

5. As no Infantry reserve stretcher bearers are available, prisoners will be used to the fullest extent to evacuate stretcher cases. O.C., A.D.S. will see that stretchers brought down by them are quickly returned to the Relay Posts.

6. Attention of all is called to Paras. 3, 4, and 5 and 6 of R.A.M.C. Operation Order No. 18.

7. <u>Locations.</u>

A.D.M.S. Office - E.28.b.5.5. (after 1400 delivery.)
A.D.S. - - - - - F.25.a.3.7.
H.Q., 155th and 157th Inf. Bdes. - - - F.30.a.5.3.
H.Q., 156th Inf. Bde. - - - - - - - - F.26.d.9.5.

8. Os.C., 1/1st and 1/2nd Low. Fld. Ambs will notify this office on completion of reliefs.

9. ACKNOWLEDGE.

Issued at 0900.

G W Brown Major
for Colonel, A.M.S.,
A.D.M.S., 52nd (Lowland) Division.

Copy No. 1 to. ~~1/1st L. F. A.~~
2 1/2nd L.F.A.
3 1/3rd L.F.A.
4. "A" & "Q"
5 "G"
6 155th Inf. Bde.
7 156th Inf. Bde.
8 157th Inf. Bde.
9 C.R.A., 52nd Divn.
10 D.D.M.S., XVII Corps.
11 Diary.
12 Diary.
13 File.
14 ADMS 57th Divn.
15 ADMS 63rd (R.N.) Divn.

Army Form A. 2007.

CENTRAL REGISTRY.

Central Registry No. and Date.	Attached Files.
Confidential	

SUBJECT, AND OFFICE OF ORIGIN.

A. D. M. S
52nd Division
War Diary – October, 1918

Referred to	Date	Referred to	Date	Referred to	Date
		VOLUME X			

P. A.	Date

Schedule of Correspondence.

Oct 1918

(12489) W6101/P773 1,000,000 3/18 W. P. & Co. (2814).

Instructions regarding War Diaries and Intelligence Summaries are contained in F. S. Regs., Part II. and the Staff Manual respectively. Title pages will be prepared in manuscript.

WAR DIARY
or
INTELLIGENCE SUMMARY.
(Erase heading not required.)

Army Form C. 2118.

Place	Date	Hour	Summary of Events and Information	Remarks and references to Appendices
Graincourt	1/10/18		ADMS Office now situated in this village at Rear Headquarters. 1/1 L.F.A. located E28 c 65 complete & in reserve, ready to carry on present A.D.S., should the latter be moved forward in the event of an advance. 1/2 L.F.A. H.Qrs at Anneux, but A.D.S. has been pushed forward to Cantaing F28 d 49. Owing to site of car post being too near bridge over Canal & consequent shelling, this has been moved some little distance.	
	2/10/18		Some 900 cases passed through A.D.S. during 12 hours ending 6 am today.	
	3/10/18		Car Post pushed forward to F30 a 42, over the canal.	
	4/10/18		Cases coming through A.D.S. in good numbers – caused by heavy shelling & M.Gs from houses in Cambrai.	

D. D & L., London, E.C. (A8004) Wt W1771/M2031 750,000 5/17 Sch. 52 Forms/C2118/14

Instructions regarding War Diaries and Intelligence Summaries are contained in F. S. Regs., Part II. and the Staff Manual respectively. Title pages will be prepared in manuscript.

WAR DIARY
or
INTELLIGENCE SUMMARY.
(*Erase heading not required.*)

Army Form C. 2118.

Place	Date	Hour	Summary of Events and Information	Remarks and references to Appendices
	5/10/18		Warning order from "G" received — Divn will be relieved tonight & concentrate West of Canal du Nord.	
	6/10/18		All Ambces now located J 9 d. area & ready for entrainment. Instructions regarding entrainment issued 2130.	
	7/10/18		ADMS Office located in Chateau at Le Couroy.	
	8/10/18		1/1 L.F.A. located at Villers Sir Simon. 1/2 L.F.A. at Blavincourt 1/3 at Ambrines. There is no accomodation for retaining slightly sick men except at 1/2 L.F.A. where 50–100 patients could be kept.	
	9/10/18		Inspected 1/6 & 1/7 H.L.I. as regards sanitation. All Baths in area examined & found in good working order.	
	10/10/18		Epidemic of Foot & Mouth Disease reported from Izel les Hameau. Area inspected & suggestions as to prevention of spreading to Military personnel made to Divisional Headquarters.	

D. D. & L., London, E.C.
(A8004) Wt W1771/M2031 750,000 5/17 Sch. 52 Forms/C2118/14

Instructions regarding War Diaries and Intelligence Summaries are contained in F. S. Regs., Part II. and the Staff Manual respectively. Title pages will be prepared in manuscript.

WAR DIARY
or
INTELLIGENCE SUMMARY.
(Erase heading not required.)

Army Form C. 2118.

Place	Date	Hour	Summary of Events and Information	Remarks and references to Appendices
	11/10/18		One tent subdivision from 1/1 L.F.A. sent to No 6 C.C.S.	
	12/10/18		Visited 11 Stat Hosp St Pol & made arrangements for [illegible] of Ear Eye & Dental cases. 1/1 L.F.A. took over Ambce site at Les Quatre Vents today.	
	13/10		Remainder of 1/1 L.F.A. moved to Les 4 Vents which is now ready to receive patients. This ambce now acting as Div Rest Station	
	14/10/18		Inspection of 1/6 & 1/7 R. Scots.	
	15/10/18		Inspection of 1/4 KOSB 1/4 & 1/5 R.S.F. ADMS visited 1/1 L.F.A. at Les 4 Vents & Skin Centre at Estree Cauchie	
	16/10/18		Sectn of 1/3 L.F.A. sent to take over & run Corps Skin Centre. Orders received from D.D.M.S. to hold 1 Motor Ambce with officers & orderlies & 1 M.O. in readiness to proceed at a moments notice to a destination to be notified later.	

D. D. & L., London, E.C.
(A8c04) Wt W1771/M2031 750,000 5/17 Sch. 52 Forms/C2118/14

Instructions regarding War Diaries and Intelligence Summaries are contained in F. S. Regs., Part II. and the Staff Manual respectively. Title pages will be prepared in manuscript.

WAR DIARY
or
INTELLIGENCE SUMMARY.
(Erase heading not required.)

Army Form C. 2118.

Place	Date	Hour	Summary of Events and Information	Remarks and references to Appendices
	17/10/18		Inspected Reception Camp. Arranged to have Disinfector moved from 156 Bde area to that of 155 Bde in view of complaints from RMOs of latter Bde to the effect ~~that~~ "clean" clothes issued at baths are verminous in some cases.	
	18/10/18		Orders received during night to send specially equipped car with MO to Douai. Orders received ref move of Division tomorrow. ADMS Op Order No 20 issued.	× App No 1
	19/10/18		This office moved to & opened at Chateau de la Haie at 1300 today. Moves ordered in O.O. No 20 completed according to time. Orders received that Divn would continue forward movement tomorrow & be located in [illegible] area.	
	20/10/18		This office opened at Cite Armand Doisen, near Henin Lietard at 1300 today. Hospital Darcy taken over & occupied by 1/2 L F A. This building is found to be in fairly good repair & capable of accomodating several hundreds of patients. It was however found to be contaminated by Mustard Gas in the cellars. On advice of Gas Officer all exits from cellars have been	

D. D. & L., London, E.C. (A8c04) Wt W1771/M2031 750,000 5/17 Sch. 52 Forms/C2118/14

Army Form C. 2118.

WAR DIARY
or
INTELLIGENCE SUMMARY.
(Erase heading not required.)

Instructions regarding War Diaries and Intelligence Summaries are contained in F. S. Regs., Part II. and the Staff Manual respectively. Title pages will be prepared in manuscript.

Place	Date	Hour	Summary of Events and Information	Remarks and references to Appendices
			sealed & no danger seems now to exist.	
			Ambce moved in Bde Groups under Bde arrangements.	
	21/10/18		The Inf Bdes moved today to area just West of Canal Haute Deule, running through Douai. German Hospital sites reconnoitred yesterday by DADMS were occupied by [illegible] Ambce HQs of 1/2 L.F.A. remain in Hospital Douai to treat & hold up slight cases.	
			Orders issued for move of 1/1 L.F.A. from Les 4 Vents to relieve 1/2 L.F.A. returned by Signals as not delivered	
	22/10/18		Orders again issued during night for move of 1/1 L.F.A. to [illegible] at [illegible], thence to Hospl Douai tomorrow	
			This Office moved to Maison de Laroche at noon.	
			All evacuations still have to be sent to Agnez les Duisans which necessitates very long journeys for cars, taking 6 hours for one journey.	

A 00 W: 1 71/M2031 750,000 5/17 Sch. 52 Forms C2118/14 London, E.

Instructions regarding War Diaries and Intelligence Summaries are contained in F. S. Regs., Part II. and the Staff Manual respectively. Title pages will be prepared in manuscript.

WAR DIARY
or
INTELLIGENCE SUMMARY.
(Erase heading not required.)

Army Form C. 2118.

Place	Date	Hour	Summary of Events and Information	Remarks and references to Appendices
Blanc Maison	23/10		Warning order received to effect that Divn would move Eastwards tomorrow. Sites for F. Ambces reconnoitred in Rache, Flines and Coutiches. All available Motor Ambces Horsed Ambces ordered to St Amand to evacuate civilians wounded. ADMS Office moved to Flines today.	
Flines	24		1/1 LFA less Tent subdivision which remains at Hénin Liétard, rejoins its affiliated Bde. Visited ADMS 8th Div to ascertain sites of ambces & evacuation routes. Visited ADMS 12th Div for same purpose.	
	25		Tent subdivision ordered to Douai by DDMS to assist in treating civilian population of villages near front line who have been wounded or sick. Epidemic of Influenza prevalent amongst civil population in this area. Cases in Division are not numerous so far.	
	26		Orders received re relief of 12th Divn. 155 & 156 Bdes move forward with 1/1 & 1/2 LFA tomorrow. O.O. No 21 issued.	Appendix 102
	27		1/1 LFA with Bde at [illegible], 1/2 LFA at Landas, 1/3 LFA remains at Rache.	

A oo , W[illegible] 1 71/M2031 750,000 5/17 Sch. 52 Forms C2[illegible]/14 London, E.

Army Form C. 2118.

Instructions regarding War Diaries and Intelligence Summaries are contained in F. S. Regs., Part II. and the Staff Manual respectively. Title pages will be prepared in manuscript.

WAR DIARY
or
INTELLIGENCE SUMMARY.
(*Erase heading not required.*)

Place	Date	Hour	Summary of Events and Information	Remarks and references to Appendices
	28/10/18		Relief of 12th Div in the line now complete — 156 Bde holding the line with 157 in support at [illegible] 155 Bde in Landas. 1/1 L.F.A. responsible for evacuating cases from front line & Support Bde. This is being done by use of wheeled stretchers & [illegible] Ambce to Ambce HQrs, thence to CCS by MAC. 1/2 L.F.A. complete in forward position, ready to push forward at short notice. 1/3 L.F.A. at Landas, treating sick of 155 Bde.	
Sameon	29/10/18		ADMS Office moved to Sameon at [illegible] today.	
	30/10/18		Extra accomodation for treatment of Influenza cases [illegible]. Influenza very prevalent amongst civilian population.	
	31/10/18		On an average of 8 or 9 cases in the Division per day [illegible]. Gargling with Pot Permang. suggested to [illegible].	

[illegible signature]

D. D. & L., London, E.C.
(A8604) Wt W1771/M2031 750,000 5/17 Sch. 52 Forms/C2118/14

Appendix I

R.A.M.C. Operation Order No. 20.
by
~~Reference~~ A.D.M.S., 52nd. Division. 18th. October, 1918.

Reference Warning Order S.R.409 of even date.

Moves. 1. O.C. 1/1st. Low. Fld. Ambce. will send 2 Bearer Sub-Divisions with 1 Officer, 3 Horsed Ambulance Wagons, 1 Limber, to report to 156th. Brigade Headquarters, at CHATEAU de la HAIE at 1500 on 19/10/18.

2. O.C. 1/2nd. Low. Fld. Ambce. will get into touch with Headquarters of 156 and 157 Brigade as to orders for move of these Brigades.
1/2nd. Low. Fld. Ambce. less 1 Section will march under orders of 157 Brigade. O.C. 1/2nd. Low. Fld. Ambce. will attach 1 Section of his Ambulance to march with 156 Brigade also two horsed Ambulance wagons (sent to him by O.C. 1/3rd. L.F.A.) and he will be responsible for the collection and evacuation of sick from 156 and 157 Brigades.

3. O.C. 1/3rd. L.F.A. will send 2 Horsed Ambulance Wagons to report to O.C. 1/2nd. L.F.A. on 19th. instant to accompany 156 Brigade. Details to be arranged between O.Cs. 1/2nd. and 1/3rd. L.F.A.
1/3rd. L.F.A. (less 1 Section at Corps Skin Centre) will move under orders of 155 Brigade. O.C. will arrange for collection and evacuation of sick of 155 Brigade.

Motor Transport. Motor Ambulance Cars will move independently by road to the Field Ambulance destinations. O.C. 1/3rd. L.F.A. will detail a car to report to A.D.M.S. Office Le CAUROY at 1100 on 19th. instant.

Sick. Sick during the move of the Division will be sent to Divisional Rest Station at Les Quatre Vents by Motor Ambces.

ACKNOWLEDGE.

[signature]

Colonel, A.M.S.,
18/10/18. A.D.M.S., 52nd. (Lowland) Division.

Issued 2000.

Appendix II

SECRET. Copy No.

R.A.M.C. OPERATION ORDER No. 71
by
A.D.M.S., 52nd (Lowland) Division.

27th October, 19[illegible].

1. The Division will relieve the 18th Division in the line to-morrow, 28th instant.
15[illegible]th Inf. Bde. will relieve [illegible]th Inf. Bde. on 28th inst. and 157th Inf. Bde. will move to [illegible] same day and remain in Divisional Support.
155th Inf. Bde. moves same day to [illegible] Area and will remain in Divisional Reserve.

From 1800 on the 28th instant, the Field Ambulances will cease to be administered by their respective Brigades and will come under this office for administration at the same hour.

2. (a) O.C., 1/1st Low. Fld. Amb. will on 28th inst. relieve and occupy M.D.S. at O.8.a.4.1. and A.D.S. at I.36.a. at present in use by 56th Field Ambulance.
He will be responsible for the evacuation of casualties of the Bde. in the front line, and also of any casualties brought to his A.D.S. by the Bearer Officer of the Bde. in Support.
(b) O.C., 1/2nd Low. Fld. Amb. will [illegible] move from [illegible] and occupy site of Headquarters, [illegible] Fld. Amb. at [illegible] on 28th instant.
He will attach one Bearer Section (including one Officer) to 157th Bde. before that Bde. moves to the Support Area. The Bearer Officer will be responsible for evacuating sick and wounded of his Brigade to A.D.S. at I.36.a.
(c) O.C., 1/3rd Low. Fld. Amb. will move to [illegible] and occupy site vacated by 1/2nd Low. Fld. Amb. on 28th.
He will be responsible for evacuating sick from the 155th Inf. Bde.
He will send one Officer in a Motor Ambulance to report for temporary duty to O.C., 1/1st Low. Fld. Amb. This officer should report, on his way, to this office [illegible], at a time to be notified later. On arrival at 1/1st Low. Fld. Amb. the Motor Ambulance Car will return to 1/3rd Low. Fld. Amb.

3. Locations of Field Ambulance Headquarters will be wired to O.C., No. [illegible] M.A.C.

4. This office will move [illegible], to [illegible] on 28th inst. opening there at 0900.

5. Exact locations will be reported to this office by Os.C., Field Ambulances on completion of moves.

6. ACKNOWLEDGE.

Issued at 1415.

Colonel, A.M.S.,
A.D.M.S., 52nd (Lowland) Division.

Copy No. 1 to 1/1st L.F.A.
2 1/2nd L.F.A.
3 1/3rd L.F.A.
4 H.Q., 52nd Divn.
5 A.D.M.S., 52nd Divn.

Confidential.

War Diary

of

A.D.M.S. 52nd (Lowland) Division.

From 1st Novr. to 30th Novr. 1918.

(Volume. XI.)

Instructions regarding War Diaries and Intelligence Summaries are contained in F. S. Regs., Part II. and the Staff Manual respectively. Title pages will be prepared in manuscript.

WAR DIARY
or
~~INTELLIGENCE~~ SUMMARY.
(Erase heading not required.)

Army Form C. 2118.

Sheet I

Place	Date	Hour	Summary of Events and Information	Remarks and references to Appendices
Jamoir	1/11/18		Attack on Valenciennes by Corps on right. No infantry action on the Divl front. Conference at DDMS office re Influenza [illegible]	
	2/11/18		Information received that enemy may retire on this front last night not confirmed.	
			Orders recd to effect that on night of 3rd the Divn would take over part of line held by Divn on the immediate right. No alteration of sites of A.D.S. reqd.	
	3/11/18		In event of enemy withdrawal this Divn will at once follow. F.A.s will remain in present sites [illegible] push forward & evacuate cases to M.D.S. [illegible]	Appendix I
	4/11/18		R.A.M.C. O.O. issued. Visited ADMS 6th Div & arranged relief. No accomodation for Influenza cases available in the F.Amb sites. Cases few in the Divn compared with others. Probab	

D. D. & L., London, E.C. (A8004) Wt W1771/M2031 750,000 5/17 Sch. 52 Forms/C2118/14

Instructions regarding War Diaries and Intelligence Summaries are contained in F. S. Regs., Part II. and the Staff Manual respectively. Title pages will be prepared in manuscript.

WAR DIARY
or
INTELLIGENCE SUMMARY.
(Erase heading not required.)

Army Form C. 2118.

Sheet 2

Place	Date	Hour	Summary of Events and Information	Remarks and references to Appendices
	5/11/18		Difficulty in finding suitable sites for Baths has been experienced lately owing to the enemy evidently not using such in this area. The only site found is in St Almond & it has been rendered useless before the enemy retreated. Pressure has been brought from time to time on the CRE to erect suitable Baths for the Division. Pressure has also been brought on "Q" Branch in reference to "Chilled Feet" & its prevention. Owing to approach of winter & the wet weather it is considered time that this matter be taken in hand seriously.	
	6/11/18		Dentist has now arrived to treat cases of the Divn – a much needed thing.	
	7/11/18		Intimation recd that no further diagnoses of P.U.O. were to be made, all such cases being returned under the heading of "Influenza"	

D. D. & L., London, E.C.
(A5004) Wt W1771/M2031 750,000 5/17 Sch. 52 Forms/C2118/14

Instructions regarding War Diaries and Intelligence Summaries are contained in F. S. Regs., Part II. and the Staff Manual respectively. Title pages will be prepared in manuscript.

WAR DIARY
or
~~INTELLIGENCE SUMMARY.~~
(Erase heading not required.)

Army Form C. 2118.

Sheet 3.

Place	Date	Hour	Summary of Events and Information	Remarks and references to Appendices
	8/10		At 0830 intimation was received that enemy had withdrawn on our front. An advanced A.D.S. was immediately opened at Haute Rive & advanced Car Posts pushed forward. RAMC O.O. No 24 issued re move of H.Q. of 2nd & 3rd L.F.A.'s & change in route of evacuation as necessitated by situation.	Appendix II
	9/10		1/1 L.F.A. moving to P17 b88. 1/2 L.F.A. now pushed forward to K23 c, keeping in touch with Bearer Officer of 156 Bde. 1/3 L.F.A. moved to Rieux de Condé (K35 b) & keeping in touch with the Bearer Officer of 157 Bde. Advance of Division progressing well, though hampered by demolition of bridges & roads. Few if any casualties are being admitted. A.D.M.S. Office moved to Mont le Peruwelz.	
	10/10		A.D.M.S. Office moved to Sirault. 1/1 L.F.A. now at Boussu[illegible]. 1/2 L.F.A. moved to Sirault & in touch with Bearer Officer 156 Bde. 1/3 L.F.A. at Hautrage.	
	11/10	0700	155 Bde with 1/3 L.F.A. moved forward from reserve, passed through & so relieved 156 Bde.	

D. D. & L., London, E.C.
(A8co4) Wt W1771/M2031 750,000 5/17 Sch. 52 Forms/C2118/14

Instructions regarding War Diaries and Intelligence Summaries are contained in F. S. Regs., Part II. and the Staff Manual respectively. Title pages will be prepared in manuscript.

WAR DIARY
or
~~INTELLIGENCE SUMMARY.~~
(*Erase heading not required.*)

Army Form C. 2118.

Sheet 4

Place	Date	Hour	Summary of Events and Information	Remarks and references to Appendices
	11th	1100	Hostilities ceased at this hour & troops will not move beyond points reached until further orders	
	13th		Information received that this Divn would be transferred to XXII Corps by 1800 on 15th and proceed to the Rhine in due course.	
	14th		Inspected units of 157 Bde & found sanitation being conducted on peacetime grounds but well.	
	15th		Official entry into Mons by Army Commander at 1030 today. Units of the Divn were represented.	
	16th		Inspected Sct Train, & Reception Camp where all parties going on leave have clothes disinfected in Foden Lorry & boots soaked in Cresol – in view of the prevalence of Foot & Mouth Disease.	
	17th		M. Officers with F. Ambces now reduced to 6, in the case of Divisions proceeding to Germany.	

D. D. & L., London, E.C.
(A8094) Wt W1771/M2031 750,000 5/17 Sch. 52 Forms/C2118/14

Instructions regarding War Diaries and Intelligence Summaries are contained in F. S. Regs., Part II. and the Staff Manual respectively. Title pages will be prepared in manuscript.

WAR DIARY
or
~~INTELLIGENCE SUMMARY.~~
(Erase heading not required.)

Army Form C. 2118.

Sheet 5

Place	Date	Hour	Summary of Events and Information	Remarks and references to Appendices
18			This office moved from Sirault to Nimy, on the outskirts of Mons.	
19			Inspected units of 156 Bde in response to complaint from BHQ that present shallow trench type of latrine was not found satisfactory. The difficulty was found to be lack of space. Suggested that deep trenches with fly proof covers be used.	
	20		On receiving intimation of the location of German Military Baths in Nimy, these were visited & found in good condition. [illegible] notified & suggestion made that same should be put in use as early as possible. ADMS inspected 5th & 6th HLI, also 2nd [illegible]	
	21		Visited ~~155 Bde Units~~ Baths at Ghlin. Found same to be those in use by miners. Not very satisfactory	

D. D. & L., London, E.C. (A800.) Wt. W171/M2031 750,000 5/17 Sch. 52 Forms C2118/14

Instructions regarding War Diaries and Intelligence Summaries are contained in F. S. Regs., Part II. and the Staff Manual respectively. Title pages will be prepared in manuscript.

WAR DIARY
or
~~INTELLIGENCE~~ SUMMARY.

(*Erase heading not required.*)

Army Form C. 2118.

Sheet 6

Place	Date	Hour	Summary of Events and Information	Remarks and references to Appendices
	23		ADMS visited units of 155 Bde.	
	25		ADMS attended conference at office of ADMS 4th Div to arrange feeding of 500,000 refugees who are expected to return to their homes in France & Belgium.	
			DADMS visited German Baths at Lens, 3 L.A. & villages in new Divl area. Baths have been dismantled by Germans before they retreated.	
			Question of disinfection very urgent, but 'Q' branch very slow in getting on with the work.	
	26		Visited Erbaut with ref to suitable sites for D.R.S. [illegible] & also accomodation for feeding refugees. Found same very unsatisfactory	

D. D. & L., London, E.C. (A5001) Wt. W1771/M2031 750,000 5/17 Sch. 52 Forms C2118/14

Instructions regarding War Diaries and Intelligence Summaries are contained in F. S. Regs., Part II. and the Staff Manual respectively. Title pages will be prepared in manuscript.

WAR DIARY
or
~~INTELLIGENCE~~ SUMMARY.
(Erase heading not required.)

Army Form C. 2118.

Sheet 7.

Place	Date	Hour	Summary of Events and Information	Remarks and references to Appendices
June	28		ADMS inspected 56th Bde RFA & found conditions most unsatisfactory	
	29		Examination of men prior to reclassification	
	30		Inspected 7th [illegible] at [illegible]. 1/1 [illegible] moved from [illegible] to [illegible]	

H. W. Brown [illegible]

Appendix I Sheet I

SECRET. 5

O.O. No. [illegible]

OPERATION ORDERS, NO. [illegible]

By A.D.M.S., 52nd (Lowland) Division.

Reference Map – [illegible] – Sheet 1a. [illegible] November, [illegible]

INTELLIGENCE.

1[illegible] Inf. Bde. relieves [illegible] Inf. Bde. ([illegible] Divn.) in the Line to-night.

1[illegible] Inf. Bde. will move to [illegible] Area on 5th inst. and will be in Divisional Support.

MEDICAL ARRANGEMENTS.

O.C., 1/3rd Low. Fld. Amb. will take over A.D.S., [illegible] Field Ambulance at [illegible], and Car Post at [illegible] to-night, relief to be completed by 0600 on 5th instant. He will also send a holding party to H.Q., [illegible] Fld. Amb. ([illegible]) to-night, preparatory to moving his Headquarters to that site to-morrow.

He will, before moving his Headquarters, evacuate all Rest Station cases to Headquarters, 1/1st L.F.A. at [illegible] and will arrange to collect sick from 1[illegible] Inf. Bde. before that Brigade moves from [illegible] Area.

On arrival in new Area, he will be responsible for evacuating all 1[illegible] Inf. Bde. cases to his A.D.S.

O.C., 1/2nd Low. Fld. Amb. will not move his Ambulance at present and will be responsible for evacuation of sick of 1[illegible] Inf. Bde. on its arrival in [illegible] Area. Any cases evacuated will be sent to 1/1st Low. Fld. Amb.

O.C., 1/1st Low. Fld. Amb. will not move his Field Ambulance at present, but will open his Headquarters as the Divisional Rest Station, from to-morrow.

Any sick cases evacuated from [illegible] Divisional Artillery will be sent to [illegible] Field Ambulance, [illegible].

Lists of stores taken over will be sent to this office.

Completion of moves and exact map references will be reported to this office.

ACKNOWLEDGE.

[signature]

Colonel, [illegible]

A.D.M.S., 52nd (Lowland) Division.

Issued at 1[illegible]00.

Copy No. 1 to 1/1st L.F.A.
2 1/2nd L.F.A.
3 1/3rd L.F.A.
4 ✓ A.D.M.S., [illegible] Divn.
5, 6 War Diary.
7 File.

Appendix F Sheet 2.

6

[illegible].

[illegible]
by
A.D.M.S. 52nd (Lowland) Division.

[illegible]

1. Headquarters of 1/2nd Low. Fld. Amb. will [illegible]
[illegible] - [illegible].
O.C., will report when his A.D.S. [illegible] and his
Headquarters at [illegible] are open, [illegible].

2. Headquarters of 1/3rd Low. Fld. Amb. will [illegible]
A.D.S. at [illegible]. O.C., will report completion.

3. As soon as all patients at present in the [illegible]
Rest Station (except [illegible].) are evacuated, O.C., [illegible]
Fld. Amb. will send all M.A.C. Cars, [illegible], to [illegible]
[illegible]. He will at the same time inform O.C., [illegible]
1/2nd Low. Fld. Amb. at [illegible] that he has done so. The
route of evacuation will then be to [illegible] and not to [illegible].
When O.C., 1/1st Low. Fld. Amb. is satisfied that the
new route of evacuation is open, he will withdraw his [illegible]
Car Posts.
O.C., 1/1st Low. Fld. Amb. will be responsible for
evacuation of sick of [illegible] Inf. Bde.
O.C., 1/1st Low. Fld. Amb. will report when the D.R.S.
is closed.

4. O.C., 1/3rd Low. Fld. Amb. will assist O.C., 1/2nd Low.
Fld. Amb. ~~[illegible]~~, with [illegible] if necessary, on application.

[signature]

Issued at [illegible] Colonel, R.A.M.C.,
12[illegible]. A.D.M.S., 52nd (Lowland) Division.

Copy No. 1 to 1/1st L.F.A.
2 1/2nd L.F.A.
3 1/3rd L.F.A.
4 [illegible]
5 Diary.
6 [illegible]
7 File.

A.D.M.S.
52nd DIV
SR 18
Date..........

Dec. 1918

Confidential.

17

War Diary

of

A.D.M.S. 52nd Division.

From 1st To 31st Decmbr 1918

(Volume. 12.)

9

14073479

Instructions regarding War Diaries and Intelligence Summaries are contained in F. S. Regs., Part II. and the Staff Manual respectively. Title pages will be prepared in manuscript.

WAR DIARY

or

~~INTELLIGENCE SUMMARY.~~

(Erase heading not required.)

Sheet I

Army Form C. 2118.

Place	Date	Hour	Summary of Events and Information	Remarks and references to Appendices
Nimy	1/12/18		Upon receiving order from DDMS XXII Corps last night, I proceeded to arrange the formation of suitable feeding & medical attention rooms at Mons Station. 2/1 L Amb to detail 2 sections to proceed to the station at dawn tomorrow.	[illegible]
	2/12/18		Station visited, met DDMS who stated his views on method of running such an establishment. Large numbers of refugees & released prisoners of war expected today	[illegible]
	3/12/18		One Tent Subdivision ordered to be sent to Cavalry Barracks, Mons, to feed & treat released prisoners of War.	[illegible]
	5/12/18		Two sections of 1/3 L.F.A. ordered to occupy the Convent de Ursulines, Mons, and act as C.C.S till 4th Canadian C.C.S can occupy the site. This establishment was ready for & received	[illegible]

D. D. & L., London, E.C.
A5001) Wt. W1771/M2031 750,000 5/17 Sch. 52 Forms C2118/14

Instructions regarding War Diaries and Intelligence Summaries are contained in F. S. Regs., Part II. and the Staff Manual respectively. Title pages will be prepared in manuscript.

WAR DIARY
or
~~INTELLIGENCE SUMMARY.~~

(Erase heading not required.)

Army Form C. 2118.

Sheet 2

Place	Date	Hour	Summary of Events and Information	Remarks and references to Appendices
			300 cases by 7 pm. Serious shortage of Med. Officers in the Divn due to amount of "Corps work" required to be done by F. Amb personnel of this Divn, and number of MOs due leave. Large numbers (2500 in 24 hours) of refugees and prisoners (800) fed by ½ L.F.A. at Mons Station during past 24 hours.	
	6/12/18		ADMS visited ⅓ L.F.A. at Mons; found that they had admitted 414 cases up from on previous evening; 224 were evacuated by Lorries to Valenciennes owing to shortage of Motor Ambce Cars. Orders received to the effect that Maj Brown DADMS, should proceed & report forthwith to ADASTRAL HOUSE, London.	
	7/12/18		Dental arrangements made for Divn with Dental Surgeon att.d No 1 C.C.S Mons.	
			Major F. W. C. Brown D.A.D.M.S. proceeded to England in accordance with orders received. Capt. H. W. Scott Wilson RAMC	

D. D. & L., London, E.C.
(A8001) Wt. W1771/M2031 750,000 5/17 Sch. 52 Forms C2.118/14

Army Form C. 2118.

Instructions regarding War Diaries and Intelligence Summaries are contained in F. S. Regs., Part II. and the Staff Manual respectively. Title pages will be prepared in manuscript.

WAR DIARY
or
~~INTELLIGENCE SUMMARY.~~

(Erase heading not required.)

Sheet 3

Place	Date	Hour	Summary of Events and Information	Remarks and references to Appendices
	7/12/18		temporarily took over duties of D.A.D.M.S.	
			Two sections of 1/3 Lowland Field Ambulance at the Convent d'Ursulines MONS handed over to the 4th Canadian C.C.S., on evening of 6/12/18, and rejoined their section at LENS (Hainault)	[initials]
	8/12/18		Circular memo. R828/2 on Sanitation issued to all Medical Officers.	AH. 1
	9/12/18		D.D.M.S. 22nd Corps. inspected Divisional Rest Station of 1/3 Lowland Field Ambulance at LENS. (Hainault).	
			A.D.M.S. attended Conference at 155 Brigade H.Q., on "Future Policy".	[initials]
	11/12/18		Party of 2 N.C.O.s and 20 Privates with 1 G.S. Wagon from 1/1 Lowland Field Ambulance, LOUVIGNIES, ~~detailed to~~ proceeded to MONS, to assist 1/2 Lowland Field Ambulance at MONS STATION.	[initials]
			A.D.M.S. visited Monastery at MASNUY-ST-PIERRE with a view to	

D. D. & L., London, E.C. (A5003) Wt. W1771/M2031 750,000 5/17 Sch. 52 Forms C2118/14

Instructions regarding War Diaries and Intelligence Summaries are contained in F. S. Regs., Part II. and the Staff Manual respectively. Title pages will be prepared in manuscript.

WAR DIARY
or
~~INTELLIGENCE SUMMARY.~~
(Erase heading not required.)

Army Form C. 2118.

Sheet 4

Place	Date	Hour	Summary of Events and Information	Remarks and references to Appendices
			determine if it was suitable for a Divisional Rest Station. The accomodation available was found to be insufficient.	
	12/12/18		O.C. 1/3 Lowland Field Ambulance and two sections proceeded to take over N.E. end of ECOLE NORMALE, MONS, to act as C.C.S., under instructions from D.D.M.S. 22nd Corps.	[initials]
	13/12/18		1/3 Lowland Field Ambulance opened as C.C.S at ECOLE NORMALE, MONS., at 09.00.	[initials]
	14/12/18		One N.C.O. and 20 Privates of 1/1 Lowland Field Ambulance transferred for temporary duty with 1/3 Lowland Field Ambulance at MONS.	[initials]
	16/12/18		1/2 Lowland Field Ambulance at MONS Station visited. Only one small train of refugees arrived during day.	

D. D. & L., London, E.C. (A7001) Wt. W1771/M2031 750,000 5/17 Sch. 52 Forms C2118/14

Instructions regarding War Diaries and Intelligence Summaries are contained in F. S. Regs., Part II. and the Staff Manual respectively. Title pages will be prepared in manuscript.

WAR DIARY
or
~~INTELLIGENCE SUMMARY.~~
(Erase heading not required.)

Army Form C. 2118.

Sheet 5

Place	Date	Hour	Summary of Events and Information	Remarks and references to Appendices
	19/12/18		Two officers withdrawn from Cavalry Barracks MONS and sent for temporary duty, one to 1/2 Lowland Field Ambulance, and one to 1/3 Lowland Field Ambulance. Twenty O.R. remain at Cavalry Barracks to feed and ~~treat~~ returning Prisoners of War.	
			The Ecole Moyenne and the Ecole professionale des Jeunes Filles, MONS taken over by parties from 1/3 Lowland Field Ambulance for the formation of a 22nd Corps Rest Station. This is also to be used as a Divisional Rest Station. Estimated accomodation of the two buildings — 200.	
			These two buildings were found to be in a very dirty condition, and a great deal of work required to render them fit for use.	[illegible initials]

D. D. & L., London, E.C. (A^{\circ}001) Wt. W1-71/M2031 750,000 5/17 Sch. 52 Forms C2..8/14

Instructions regarding War Diaries and Intelligence Summaries are contained in F. S. Regs., Part II. and the Staff Manual respectively. Title pages will be prepared in manuscript.

WAR DIARY
or
~~INTELLIGENCE SUMMARY.~~
(Erase heading not required.)

Army Form C. 2118.

Sheet 6

Place	Date	Hour	Summary of Events and Information	Remarks and references to Appendices
	23/12/18		Corps Rest Station at Ecole Moyenne and Ecole Professionale des Jeunes Filles, MONS, received patient from 14.00.	
			Ecole Normale, MONS, which was being run as a C.C.S by 1/3 Lowland Field Ambulance, was vacated.	[initials]
	26/12/18		Major J.P. Quinn took over the duties of D.A.D.M.S. 52nd Div. Capt H.W. Scott-Wilson, temporarily performing the duties of D.A.D.M.S. resumed medical charge of 52nd Div R.E.	[initials]
	28/12/18		Col. A.J. MacDougall A.M.S. took over the duties of D.D.M.S. XXII. Corps vice Col. E.W. Bliss A.M.S. on leave.	[initials]
	30/12/18		A/DDMS inspected No. 30 C.C.S. LA LOUVIERE; 1/2 Highland F. Ambulance Bois du Luc, and No 11. F. Ambulance LA LOUVIERE	[initials]
	31/12/18		A/DDMS inspected No 1. Lowland F. Ambulance Chaussée N.D. Louvignies, No 3 Lowland	[initials]

D. D. & L., London, E.C. (A8001) Wt. W1771/M2031 750,000 5/17 Sch. 52 Forms C2118/14

Army Form C. 2118.

Instructions regarding War Diaries and Intelligence Summaries are contained in F. S. Regs., Part II. and the Staff Manual respectively. Title pages will be prepared in manuscript.

WAR DIARY
or
~~INTELLIGENCE~~ SUMMARY.

(*Erase heading not required.*)

Sheet 7.

Place	Date	Hour	Summary of Events and Information	Remarks and references to Appendices
			Field Ambulance LENS, and 2nd Lowland Field Ambulance (less 1 section) the Station, MONS, which functions as a Clearing Station for Refugees. Two to three thousand refugees pass through this station daily. Food and housing arrangements were found very efficient.	(A)
			A. J. Mac Dougall Col ADMS 5 2 Div	

D. L. London, E. A.003 W. 1 71/M2031 750,000 5/17 Sch. 52 Forms C2118/14

Appendix I Sheet 3

A.D.M.S., 53rd Divn. No. R.828/2.

Medical Officer i/c,

---

1. Now that the Division is no longer engaged in active operations and is living under more civilised conditions than when in the trenches, the major part of a R.M.O's work should be in connection with Sanitation. By Sanitation, I mean all the questions which affect the health of the Troops. It is your duty to try to prevent sick wastage in the Unit over which you hold Medical Supervision, and this can be kept low only by most careful supervision of all points which come under the heading of Sanitation.

Part II, Section 84, of Field Service Regulations lays down clearly that the O.C. of a Unit is responsible to higher authority for the Sanitation of his Unit. This does not mean that <u>you</u>, as R.M.O., are devoid of responsibility. You are the advisor of your C.O. on all questions which affect the health of the Unit, and your C.O. looks to you to keep him advised on all matters of sanitation. On visiting Units, it is noticeable that in many cases there is a want of liason between the M.O. and the C.O. or Adjutant, and, such being the case, it is difficult for an inspecting officer to know on whom to put the blame for defective sanitation.

To avoid doubt, you should make it a practice to render written suggestions and reports to your C.O., sending a duplicate to this office. A copy of same should be kept by yourself to show to any inspecting officer what steps you have taken to remedy any defects should they still exist when the latter pays his visit.

Your sanitary duties may be taken to come under 6 headings -

1. General cleanliness of the men and billets.
2. Supervision of food and cooking of same.
3. Supervision of water supply, from the source to the man.
4. Supervision of disposal of liquid waste.
5. Supervision of disposal of solid waste.
6. Prevention of spread of Infectious Disease.

2. <u>General Cleanliness of the Men and Billets.</u>

It is estimated that the following disease, all due to dirt, are the cause of three-quarters of the sick wastage - (a) Skin affections, due directly or indirectly (by scratching with dirty nails) to itch and lice, (b) All so-called Trench Fevers, now proved to be transmitted by lice, (c) Pains, debility, and a proportion of heart affections, the result of Trench Fever.

From the above, it will be understood how important personal cleanliness has become as a saver of man-power. The essential means to secure cleanliness are :- (a) Ample bathing accomodation, (b) Liberal supplies of clean underwear, (c) A system of delousing the outer clothing and blankets, (d) Weekly, and thorough, health inspections of the men.

<u>Supervision of food and clothing.</u>

You should visit the Q.M.Stores and follow the handling of the food through all the various stages, including the cooking of same. Satisfy yourself that it is kept free from dirt while in the stores, in the cook's hands, or in the man's dixie.

<u>Supervision of Water Supply.</u>

It may be taken that all unchlorinated or unboiled water is dangerous for consumption. It is your duty therefore to see that no such water is used. Careful selection of wells to be used, is necessary, paying attention to the position of any civilian latrine to the well, most of which in this country, are within a few yards of the well used by the house. The testing of the water should be done by yourself and only that water which gives the Horrock's Test in the first cup should be used.

The training of water-duty personnel and the cleanliness of the water-carts must be supervised by you.

Disposal/

Disposal of Liquid Waste.

Satisfy yourself that all drains are in good condition, that urinals are provided both for day and night use, and that no kitchen and bath-house water is allowed to collect on the surface of the ground.

Disposal of Solid Waste.

The position and type of latrine to be used should be carefully selected and examined daily for defects in maintenance. The position and type of incinerator for all other refuse must be selected by you and you should satisfy yourself ~~that~~ daily that all such refuse is burned (or tins scalded) before being put into a pit. Horse manure should be closed packed.

Infectious Disease.

The steps to be taken, in case of Infectious Disease being reported, varies somewhat with the disease; but in all cases, strict isolation of contacts, disinfection of billets, clothing etc., must be attempted.

3. The above must not be taken as the sum total of your duties, but it is only meant to be an example of the general lines to be adopted and is sent for the information of R.M.Os who may not have had long experience of Regimental Duties.

4. In conclusion, bear in mind two points :-

(a) When in doubt, ask advice from higher Medical Authority.

(b) If no good result is obtained after making written suggestions to your C.O., refer the matter to higher Medical Authority.

W J MacDougall

Colonel, A.M.S.,

9/12/18. A.D.M.S., 52nd (Lowland) Division.

* * * * * * * * * * * * * * *

Jan. 1919 17

VR 10

140/3487

Box 2749

CONFIDENTIAL.

WAR DIARY

OF

A.D.M.S. 52nd DIVISION.

FROM. 1ST. TO 31ST. JANUARY. 1919.

VOLUME 1

Army Form C. 2118.

Instructions regarding War Diaries and Intelligence Summaries are contained in F. S. Regs., Part II. and the Staff Manual respectively. Title pages will be prepared in manuscript.

WAR DIARY
or
INTELLIGENCE SUMMARY.
(Erase heading not required.)

Place	Date	Hour	Summary of Events and Information	Remarks and references to Appendices
	1/1/19		A/DDMS. inspected the Corps Rest Station, and No. 2 Lowland Field Ambulance, the Station, MONS.	
	2/1/19		A/D.D.M.S. inspected No. 42 M.A.C. MONS; No 8. Sanitary Section, MONS; and attended the Memorial Service, for the Allies fallen in the war, held at the Cathedral MONS. Arrangements made for lectures in Bacteriology to be given twice weekly, on Tuesdays and Thursdays, at MUSEE d'HYGIENE, BOULEVARDE CHARLES SAINCTLETTE, MONS, for the benefit of Medical Officers of XXII Corps.	
	3/1/19		A/DDMS inspected 1st Lowland Field Ambulance CHAUSSEE N.D. LOUVIGNIES and 4th Batt. KOSB.	
	4/1/19		A/D.D.M.S. inspected 9th and 56th Bdes R.F.A., and the new site for 155 Inf. Bde. Baths at JURBISE.	

J.P. Owen
Major RAMC
DADMS
52nd Div.

D. & L. London, E.C. A 001 Wt 171/M2031 750,000 5/17 Sch. 52 Forms C2118/14

Instructions regarding War Diaries and Intelligence Summaries are contained in F. S. Regs., Part II. and the Staff Manual respectively. Title pages will be prepared in manuscript.

WAR DIARY
or
INTELLIGENCE SUMMARY.
(Erase heading not required.)

Army Form C. 2118.

Place	Date	Hour	Summary of Events and Information	Remarks and references to Appendices
	5/1/19		A/DDMS inspected the Refugee Clearing Station MONS.	
			An application was forwarded to Sir Edward Ward, Director General of Voluntary Organizations for clothing for French and Belgian Refugees.	MC
	6/1/19		An application was forwarded for Capt W. Goldie RAMC. T.F. 2nd Lowland Field Ambulance, to be promoted A/Major vice Major D. Lamb RAMC T.F. who proceeded to England for demobilization.	MC
			Samples of wines and spirits, left behind by the retreating Germans, and believed to have been drugged by them, were received from the Town Major, MAISIERES. These wines and spirits were being sold by civilians. These samples were sent to the Base ~~[illegible]~~ Laboratory, Boulogne, for analysis. All such wines and spirits were confiscated by the Military Authorities, and the houses selling them were put "out of bounds" for all troops, pending further information.	MC
	7/1/19		The Burgomasters of LENS and MONS, requested, that the school-houses in these areas which were being temporarily used, by the Field Ambulances of the Division, as hospitals, might be vacated, to permit the re-opening of the schools.	MC

D. D. & L., London, E.C.
(A8001) Wt. W1771/M2031 750,000 5/17 Sch. 52 Forms C2118/14

Instructions regarding War Diaries and Intelligence Summaries are contained in F. S. Regs., Part II. and the Staff Manual respectively. Title pages will be prepared in manuscript.

WAR DIARY
or
INTELLIGENCE SUMMARY.
(Erase heading not required.)

Army Form C. 2118.

Place	Date	Hour	Summary of Events and Information	Remarks and references to Appendices
	8/1/19		Ceremonial parade held. The following personnel of RAMC were presented with decorations by G.O.C. Division :-	

No.	Rank	Name	Corps	Decoration	Unit
No 320187	Cpl	J.A. McC[illegible]	RAMC	M. Medal	3rd Lowland Field Ambulance
" 320041	Pte.	T.A. Pullen	"	" "	
" 320063	"	L. Horsburgh	"	" "	
" 320108	"	R.L. Watt	"	" "	
" 320223	"	G. Angus	"	" "	
" 328071	"	C.P. Lyle	"	" "	
" M1/09026	"	G.E. Hutton	A.S.C. M.T.	" "	
No 316229	Sgt.	J. McGregor	RAMC	M. Medal	1st Lowland Field Ambulance
" 316066	"	J.S. Campbell	"	" "	
" 22891	Cpl.	J Edwards	"	" "	
" 316235	Pte.	J McCartney	"	" "	
" 318164	"	E Hutton	"	" "	
" M2/135999	"	G.J. Blackwell	A.S.C. M.T.	" "	
No 318003	S/S.	J Mack		M. Medal	2nd Lowland Field Ambulance
318010	"	J Spence		" "	
318033	Sgt	J Johnson		" " and Bar	
492040	A/Sgt	H Watson		" "	
318034	Sgt	R. Stevenson		" "	
316351	Pte.	W. Getgood		" "	
318125	"	J.C. Currie		" "	
318218	"	T. Smith		" "	
T4/247029	Dr.	A Kerr		" "	
M2/135961	Pte.	M. Bailey		" "	
M2/020454	"	G. Morton		" "	
M2/033543	"	N. Fulsham		" "	

D. D. & L., London, E.C.
(A5001) Wt. W1-71/M2031 750,000 5/17 Sch. 52 Forms C2118/14

Army Form C. 2118.

Instructions regarding War Diaries and Intelligence Summaries are contained in F. S. Regs., Part II. and the Staff Manual respectively. Title pages will be prepared in manuscript.

WAR DIARY
or
INTELLIGENCE SUMMARY.
(Erase heading not required.)

Place	Date	Hour	Summary of Events and Information	Remarks and references to Appendices
	9/1/19		Leave to Brussels opened: 72 hours leave of absence granted. Allotment for R.A.M.C., 4 O.R. per day.	[initials]
	10/1/19		A/D.D.M.S. inspected 2nd Lowland Field Ambulance, MONS. A/Major J. Browne R.A.M.C. 1st Lowland Field Ambulance, proceeded to England for demobilization, and relinquishes the acting rank of Major from to-day.	
	11/1/19		Notification received that First Army Opthalmic Centre will be closed until 1/2/19, except for very urgent cases.	[initials]
	12/1/19		A/D.D.M.S. inspected 5th and 6th H.L.I.	[initials]
	14/1/19		XXII. Corps Medical Society meeting held. A/D.D.M.S. presided. OC. No. 1. C.C.S. delivered a lecture on "Wound Shock". There was a good attendance of Medical Officers from the division.	[initials]
	15/1/19		The revised Establishment of a Field Ambulance received. The new Field Ambulance consisting of two sections, with personnel, 8 officers and 211 O.R.	[initials]

D. D. & L., London, E.C.
(A7001) Wt. W1771/M2031 750,000 5/17 Sch. 52 Forms C2118/14

Instructions regarding War Diaries and Intelligence Summaries are contained in F. S. Regs., Part II. and the Staff Manual respectively. Title pages will be prepared in manuscript.

WAR DIARY
or
INTELLIGENCE SUMMARY.
(Erase heading not required.)

Army Form C. 2118.

Place	Date	Hour	Summary of Events and Information	Remarks and references to Appendices
	16/1/19		Field Ambulance were instructed to hand over to No 19 Advance Depot Medical Stores the medical equipment of one tent sub-division.	MC
	16/1/19		A series of lectures on Practical Bacteriology commenced to-day, Thursday, at No 2 Mobile Laboratory, MONS. These lectures will be given every Thursday and Tuesday.	MC
	18/1/19		A/D.D.M.S. inspected 3rd Lowland Field Ambulance, MONS. and 4th and 5th R.S.F.	MC
	19/1/19		Instructions received from XXII Corps, to close the Corps Troops Rest Station at Ecole Mayenne, Mons. The 3rd Lowland Field Ambulance has functioned as the C.T.R.S.	MC
	20/1/19		3rd Lowland Field Ambulance, less cadre strength, reported to No1. C.C.S. Mons, for duty.	MC
	21/1/19		Cadre of 3rd L. F. Amb. left the Ecole Mayenne, and took over No 33 Rue de la Potterie, Mons, as billets, and stores for equipment.	MC

D. D. & L., London, E.C. (A5001) Wt. W1771/M2031 750,000 5/17 Sch. 52 Forms C2118/14

Instructions regarding War Diaries and Intelligence Summaries are contained in F. S. Regs., Part II. and the Staff Manual respectively. Title pages will be prepared in manuscript.

WAR DIARY
or
INTELLIGENCE SUMMARY.
(Erase heading not required.)

Army Form C. 2118.

Hour, Date, Place	Summary of Events and Information	Remarks and References to Appendices
21/1/19	Lecture on Bacteriology at No. 2. Mobile Laboratory, Mons. These lectures will be delivered on Mondays and Thursdays in future.	[initials]
21/1/19	1st Lowland Field Ambulance took over the D.R.S. from the 3rd Lowland Field Ambulance at LENS.	[initials]
22/1/19	A/D.D.M.S. inspected 1st Lowland Field Ambulance detachments at CHAUSSEE N.D. LOUVIGNIES and at LENS.	[initials]
	Six men of 22nd Sanitary Section were sent home to England for demobilization. These deficiencies were made up by attaching 2 O.R. from each Field Ambulance to No 22 Sanitary Section.	[initials]
23/1/19	A/D.D.M.S. inspected 4th and 7th Royal Scots and 7th Scottish Rifles.	[initials]
	Lecture on Bacteriology delivered at No 2 Mobile Laboratory MONS.	[initials]

(9 29 6) W 3332—1107 100,000 10/13 H W V Forms/C. 2118/10.

Instructions regarding War Diaries and Intelligence Summaries are contained in F. S. Regs., Part II. and the Staff Manual respectively. Title pages will be prepared in manuscript.

WAR DIARY
or
INTELLIGENCE SUMMARY.
(Erase heading not required.)

Army Form C. 2118.

Hour, Date, Place	Summary of Events and Information	Remarks and References to Appendices
25/1/19	A/D.D.M.S. inspected 2nd Lowland Field Ambulance MONS, and detachment of 1st Lowland Field Ambulance LENS.	HC
28/1/19	Clinical demonstration at No 1. C.C.S. MONS. Major W.W. Greer RAMC was released from Military Service whilst on leave to U.K. Colonel E.W. Bliss AMS, D.D.M.S XXII. Corps returned from leave. Colonel A MacDougall AMS A.D.M.S. 52nd Div, who had acted for Colonel Bliss whilst he was on leave, proceeded to U.K. on 14 days leave. Lt-Colonel J. Young RAMC O.C. 1/3 Lowland Field Ambulance took over the duties of A.D.M.S. 52nd Div.	HC
31/1/19	Extract from Gazette. "Lt. Colonel J. Young RAMC. O.C. 1/3 Lowland Field Ambulance, awarded the D.S.O. T/S.M. Weldon 3rd Lowland Field Ambulance awarded the M.S.M.	HC

Confidential

Feb 1919

War Diary

of

A.D.M.S. 52ND DIVISION

FROM 1ST. TO 28TH FEBY. 1919.

(VOLUME 2.)

24

"

VIII

109/3026

Army Form C. 2118.

Instructions regarding War Diaries and Intelligence Summaries are contained in F. S. Regs., Part II. and the Staff Manual respectively. Title pages will be prepared in manuscript.

WAR DIARY
or
~~INTELLIGENCE SUMMARY.~~
(Erase heading not required.)

Sheet 1

Hour, Date, Place	Summary of Events and Information	Remarks and References to Appendices
1/2/19	Capt H. W. SCOTT-WILSON was posted for temporary duty as D.A.D.M.S. 57th Division. D.A.D.M.S. inspected 9th and 56th Bdes R.F.A. with M.O's of these units.	[initials]
2/2/19	Conference held at office of D.D.M.S. XXII Corps. Alterations or changes in R.A.M.C. uniform discussed.	[initials]
3/2/19	Orders received to detail a Sergeant Major for duty in connection with Base Depot Medical Stores, Boulogne.	[initials]
4/2/19	A/A.D.M.S. inspected 1 Lowland Field Ambulance, detachments at CHAUSSÉE N.D. LOUVIGNIES and at LENS.	[initials]
5/2/19	A/A.D.M.S. inspected Refugee Clearing Centre, at the Station Mons, and also 3rd Lowland Field Ambulance Mons.	[initials]

(9 29 6) W 3332—1107 100,000 10/13 H W V Forms/C. 2118/10.

Instructions regarding War Diaries and Intelligence Summaries are contained in F. S. Regs., Part II. and the Staff Manual respectively. Title pages will be prepared in manuscript.

WAR DIARY
or
~~INTELLIGENCE SUMMARY.~~
(Erase heading not required.)

Army Form C. 2118.

Sheet 2

Hour, Date, Place	Summary of Events and Information	Remarks and References to Appendices
8/2/19	Official notification received that Capt McMichael RAMC was demobilised whilst on leave, 31/1/19.	[initials]
9/2/19	A/A.D.M.S. inspected M.Os of 155 Brigade Group.	[initials]
10/2/19	Arrangements made by D.D.M.S. XXII Corps, for O.Cs Sanitary Sections to visit A.D.M.Ss, and discuss matters of importance, particularly any outbreak of infectious disease.	[initials]
11/2/19	Lt-Col J. W. Leitch returned from leave and took over the duties of temporary A.D.M.S. 52nd Div.	[initials]
14/2/19	Col. A. J. MacDougall C.M.G. A.M.S. returned from leave and took over the duties of A.D.M.S. from Lt. Col. J. W. Leitch.	[initials]

(9 29 6) W 3332—1107 100,000 10/13 H W V Forms/C. 2118/10.

Army Form C. 2118.

Instructions regarding War Diaries and Intelligence Summaries are contained in F. S. Regs., Part II. and the Staff Manual respectively. Title pages will be prepared in manuscript.

WAR DIARY
or
~~INTELLIGENCE SUMMARY.~~
(Erase heading not required.)

Sheet 3

Hour, Date, Place	Summary of Events and Information	Remarks and References to Appendices
15/2/19.	Orders received from D.D.M.S. XXII Corps. (Wire A79) for Lieut. G.R. Ross. RAMC. S.R., M.O. i/c. 5th H.L.I. to report to 15th Wing R.A.F. GERPINNES (NAMUR MAP). Instructions issued regarding above move to-day.	[initials]
	D.D.M.S. XXII Corps. letter received asking if it was thought necessary to retain D.A.Ds.M.S with Divisions. The reply given was that in the best interests of the service it were well to retain this appointment in Divisions.	
	All Medical Officers were to-day informed by memo that the medical examination of men prior to proceeding on demobilization is to include examination for active signs of Venereal Disease.	
16/2/19	Demobilization orders received from DDMS XXII Corps (M1/270/168) for A/Lt. Col. J.W. Leitch D.S.O RAMC. T.F. OC. 1/1st Lowland Field Ambce and Capt. J. Allan RAMC. T.C. MO i/c 52nd D.A.C. Instructions issued to Officers concerned.	[initials]

(9 29 6) W 3332—1107 100,000 10/13 H W V Forms/C. 2118/10.

Army Form C. 2118.

Instructions regarding War Diaries and Intelligence Summaries are contained in F. S. Regs., Part II. and the Staff Manual respectively. Title pages will be prepared in manuscript.

WAR DIARY
or
~~INTELLIGENCE SUMMARY.~~
(Erase heading not required.)

Sheet 4.

Hour, Date, Place	Summary of Events and Information	Remarks and References to Appendices
14 2/19.	Lieut G.R. Ross departed to-day to report to GERPINNES, Lieut WILLIS MORC USA 1/6th HLI took over medical charge of 1/5th H.L.I in addition to his other duties.	[initials]
20 2/19	Major J.P. Quinn MC. RAMC. DADMS. 52nd Division proceeded to Aldershot to take his place in B.E.F. Rugby Team.	[initials]
	Elimination of Units and formations down to cadre establishment is now proceeding. Division will probably be concentrated at SOIGNES (about 14 Kilos N.W. of MONS) Field Ambulances have been instructed accordingly.	
22 2/19	Field Ambulances have been instructed to have all Thomas' Splints cleaned and kept in good condition. That only necessary drugs etc are to be indented for and that the indents received from Regimental Medical Officers are to be carefully scrutinized so as to avoid	[initials]

(9 29 6) W 3332—1107 100,000 10/13 H W V Forms/C. 2118/10.

Instructions regarding War Diaries and Intelligence Summaries are contained in F. S. Regs., Part II. and the Staff Manual respectively. Title pages will be prepared in manuscript.

WAR DIARY

or

~~INTELLIGENCE SUMMARY.~~

(Erase heading not required.)

Army Form C. 2118.

Sheet 5.

Hour, Date, Place	Summary of Events and Information	Remarks and References to Appendices
	waste and surplus issues.	
23.2.19	Capt. C. C. Philip, RAMC. T.F., MO i/c. 1/4th R.S.F. left to-day under orders of DDMS XXII Corps (M1/299/207 dated 13.2.19) to report for duty to D.D.M.S. ROUEN.	[initials]
	Capt. J. P. McDonald RAMC. T.C. has been promised in relief but has not yet reported.	
	52nd Divisional Reception Camp in MONS has been closed down, its services being dispensed with. The Foden Disinfector stationed there will be moved to a Central Point - JURBISE OR LENS.	
24.2.19	Capt J. Allan RAMC. T.C. MO. 52nd D.A.C. departed today for Demobilization. His unit will be medically looked after by the MO. 56th Bde R.F.A.	[initials]
	An outbreak of Typhoid has been reported in SOIGNES. Civil Authorities have been asked to segregate patients and I have called for a	

(9 29 6) W 3332—1107 100,000 10/13 H W V Forms/C. 2118/10.

Instructions regarding War Diaries and Intelligence Summaries are contained in F. S. Regs., Part II. and the Staff Manual respectively. Title pages will be prepared in manuscript.

WAR DIARY
or
~~INTELLIGENCE~~ SUMMARY.
(*Erase heading not required.*)

Army Form C. 2118.

Sheet 6.

Hour, Date, Place	Summary of Events and Information	Remarks and References to Appendices
	report from the Medical Officer of the 147 Army Brigade R.F.A. No military cases have occurred.	
25 2/19	A/Lieut Col. J. W. Leitch DSO, OC 1/1st Lowland Field Ambce departed to-day to be demobilized and relinquished A/rank. A/Major W. D. Mackenzie has taken over command of the Unit.	[initials]
26 2/19	A Letter of appreciation of the work done by the 1/2nd Lowland Field Ambulance at MONS Station in connection with the feeding and handling of French repatriated soldiers and civilians, (some 140,000 having been dealt with) received from French Mission, XXII Corps, and communicated to OC 1/2nd Lowland Field Ambce.	[initials]
27 2/19	Medical Officers instructed to destroy all records of men who have applied for Early Treatment (Venereal Disease precautions) Only numbers to be kept in future.	

Instructions regarding War Diaries and Intelligence Summaries are contained in F. S. Regs., Part II. and the Staff Manual respectively. Title pages will be prepared in manuscript.

WAR DIARY
or
~~INTELLIGENCE SUMMARY.~~
(Erase heading not required.)

Army Form C. 2118.

Sheet 7.

Hour, Date, Place	Summary of Events and Information	Remarks and references to Appendices
27/2/19	Notices sent to Div. H.Q. for distribution to Units for posting in Latrines etc warning men re Venereal Disease and the necessity for Early Treatment see appendix	Appendix No I.
28/2/19	Volunteers asked for Medical Officers to serve in NORTH RUSSIA. No volunteers from this Division.	
	Numbers R.A.M.C. ORs. Demobilized:-	
	W.E. 7/2/19. 15	
	W.E. 14/2/19 15	
	W.E. 21/2/19 16	
	W.E. 28/2/19 15	
	Total. 61	

[signature]
Colonel AMS.
ADMS. 52nd Division.

(9 29 6) W 3332—1107 100,000 10/13 H W V Forms/C. 2118/10.

APPENDIX No 1
Sheet 7.

N O T I C E.

1. EARLY TREATMENT ROOMS for Venereal Disease exist in connection with the AID POST of all Units of the 52nd (Lowland) Division - also in MONS, distinguished by a BLUE LAMP, at

21, RUE De La STATION.

11, RUE FETIS.

2. and in BRUSSELS at

Y.M.C.A. RUE NEUVE.

Canadian V. D. C. 25, RUE FOSSE AUX LOUPS.

PALAIS SOMYER HOSPITAL.

3. Apply AT ONCE at one of these immediately on running the risk of being infected.

Confidential

War Diary

of

A. D. M. S. 52nd (Low) Division

FROM 1st March to 31st March 1919

(Volume 2.)

14

WO 95/4

112

Instructions regarding War Diaries and Intelligence Summaries are contained in F. S. Regs., Part II. and the Staff Manual respectively. Title pages will be prepared in manuscript.

WAR DIARY

~~or~~

~~INTELLIGENCE SUMMARY.~~

(Erase heading not required.)

Army Form C. 2118.

Hour, Date, Place	Summary of Events and Information	Remarks and references to Appendices
NIMY, near MONS. Belgium. 1/3/19.	Address to be given to men on being demobilized see appendix.	APPENDIX I.
3/3/19.	Instructions received from 'Q' Branch, Division. Detailing 1/1st and 1/3rd Lowland Field Ambces. to send 5 horses each for Sale by Auction to SOIGNIES on 6th instant. Ambulances concerned notified accordingly.	
	Orders received from DDMS XXII Corps. (M1/339/171 d/2.3/19) for Surgeon Lieut Commander C. Ross R.N., 1/1st. L.F.AMB. to proceed to U.K. and report to Admiralty for Duty. Instructions issued.	

(9 29 6) W 3332—1107 100,000 10/13 H W V Forms/C. 2118/10.

Army Form C. 2118.

Instructions regarding War Diaries and Intelligence Summaries are contained in F. S. Regs., Part II. and the Staff Manual respectively. Title pages will be prepared in manuscript.

WAR DIARY

~~or INTELLIGENCE SUMMARY.~~

(Erase heading not required.)

Hour, Date, Place	Summary of Events and Information	Remarks and References to Appendices
3/3/19.	Orders received from D.D.M.S. XXII Corps, (M/341/171 of 2/3/19) for Capt. W. A. Todd, RAMC T.C., MO i/c 1/5th RSF to report to D.M.S. Second Army for duty. Instructions issued. Capt. H. W. K. Smith M.C. MO i/c 1/4th KOSB to take over medical charge of 1/5th RSF in addition to present duties.	[initials]
4/3/19	Under orders of D.D.M.S. XXII Corps. 115 O.Rs of 1/2nd L.F. Ambce moved out of the Station Buildings, Mons and were accommodated in other Billets in the Town. Headquarters of the Unit remain at the Station.	[initials]
5/3/19	17th Northumberland Fusiliers, Pioneer Unit of this Division, now down to Cadre Strength. The medical Officer, Capt. J Evans. RAMC T.C. has been withdrawn and posted for duty with 1/1st L. F. AMBCE, LENS. The Cadre personnel	

(9 29 6) W 3332—1107 100,000 10/13 H W V Forms/C. 2118/10.

Instructions regarding War Diaries and Intelligence Summaries are contained in F. S. Regs., Part II. and the Staff Manual respectively. Title pages will be prepared in manuscript.

WAR DIARY

~~or~~

~~INTELLIGENCE~~ ~~SUMMARY~~.

(*Erase heading not required.*)

Army Form C. 2118.

Hour, Date, Place	Summary of Events and Information	Remarks and References to Appendices
	of 17 N.F.s will be medically supervised by the M.O. 1/4 KOSB in addition to his other duties.	
	The prevalence of Enteric in SOIGNIES reported by me to the Division. Precautionary instructions recommended for issue to the troops stationed there.	[initials] See Appendix.
5 3/19.	Lieut Surgeon Commander Ross. R.N. 1/1st L.F.A. left his unit today to report to Admiralty.	[initials]
7 3/19.	Capt W. A. Dodd. RAMC. T.C. proceeded today for duty with Second Army.	
	OC. 1/1st. L.F.A. instructed to detail 1 N.C.O. and 19 ORs. RAMC to assist 1/2nd L.F.A in their work at MONS.	[initials]
10 3/19	The attention of all O.C. Medical Units has been called to G.R.O. 3311 precautions and treatment of INFLUENZA.	

(9 29 6) W 3332—1107 100,000 10/13 H W V Forms/C. 2118/10.

Instructions regarding War Diaries and Intelligence Summaries are contained in F. S. Regs., Part II. and the Staff Manual respectively. Title pages will be prepared in manuscript.

WAR DIARY
or
~~INTELLIGENCE SUMMARY.~~
(Erase heading not required.)

Army Form C. 2118.

Hour, Date, Place	Summary of Events and Information	Remarks and References to Appendices
11/3/19	Circular regarding reporting of Scabies cases and the necessity of regular inspection, by medical Officers, of men in Units sent out to all concerned.	[initials] See Appendix
13/3/19.	Re-distribution of medical Officers. D.M.S. First Army considers the following scale should meet the Division's needs while in process of Demobilization. 1. O.C. and 1 Quartermaster per Field Ambce. 6 medical Officers for other Units of the Division. Numbers surplus to above furnished to D.D.M.S XXII Corps for re-posting to other formations.	
	Capt. J. W. Burton RAMC. M.O./c 1/4th Royal Scots Detailed to proceed to U.K and to report War Office for service in INDIA.	[initials]

(9 29 6) W 3332—1107 100,000 10/13 H W V Forms/C. 2118/10.

Instructions regarding War Diaries and Intelligence Summaries are contained in F. S. Regs., Part II. and the Staff Manual respectively. Title pages will be prepared in manuscript.

WAR DIARY

~~or~~

~~INTELLIGENCE SUMMARY.~~

(Erase heading not required.)

Army Form C. [illegible]118.

Hour, Date, Place	Summary of Events and Information	Remarks and References to Appendices
16/3/19	Capt. A/major W.F. Mackenzie departs to be demobilized 19/3/19 Authority Deported Wire DM 137 (AMD1) 1/3/19. Orders issued.	[initials]
19/3/19	Capt. A/Lieut Col. D.J. Scott. MC. 1/2nd Lowland Field Ambce departed today for demobilization authority Deported Wire MM 191. 4 3/19. Relinquished A/Rank.	[initials]
19 3/19	Lieut H.W. Gwynn MORC USA 1/2nd L.F.AMB. posted to 50th (S.A) Bde R.G.A Capt H. Webb joins in relief and was posted to 1/7 HL1.	[initials]
20 3/19	Capt. W. Goldie 1/2nd L.F.A. Evacuated to Base Sick 26/2/19 Relinquishes A/rank of Major from 21/1/19 on Field Ambces being reduced to 2 Sections.	[initials]

(9 29 6) W 3332—1107 100,000 10/13 H W V Forms/C. 2118/10.

Instructions regarding War Diaries and Intelligence Summaries are contained in F. S. Regs., Part II. and the Staff Manual respectively. Title pages will be prepared in manuscript.

WAR DIARY

~~or~~

~~INTELLIGENCE SUMMARY.~~

(*Erase heading not required.*)

Army Form C. 2118.

Hour, Date, Place	Summary of Events and Information	Remarks and References to Appendices
21/3/19	Capt. W.E.K. Coles 1/3rd ?. A. posted to 21st. mobile Laboratory to-day.	[initials]
21/3/19	Orders received that Division will concentrate at SOIGNIES for entrainment of Cadres - Division to be ready commence entraining on 25th. Ambulances warned to move Accommodation arranged at THE CONVENT, SOIGNIES.	[initials]
21/3/19	Capt. S.J. Nunn MORC. U.S.A. 9th Bde R.F.A. posted to 147th Bde R.F.A. and Capt. H.L Warren-Woodrofe posted to 9th Bde R.F.A.	[initials]
21/3/19	Orders received for Demobilization of Capt. A. D. Downes 1/1st L.F.A. This Officer is at present on leave. Instructions issued for his departure on return from leave,	[initials]

Instructions regarding War Diaries and Intelligence Summaries are contained in F. S. Regs., Part II. and the Staff Manual respectively. Title pages will be prepared in manuscript.

WAR DIARY

or

~~INTELLIGENCE SUMMARY.~~

(*Erase heading not required.*)

Army Form C. 2118.

Hour, Date, Place	Summary of Events and Information	Remarks and References to Appendices
22/3/19	Move of Field Ambces to the CONVENT completed. OC. 1/3rd L.F.A has been appointed S.M.O medical Units. for purpose of administration. A.D.M.S. Office ceases to exist after 25/3/19.	[initials]
22/3/19	Four Talbot Ambulance Cars complete to proceed to DOUAI dispatched to M.T. Workshops Ahlin.	[initials]
22/3/19	Capt. J Evans 1/1st L.F.A. Detailed to take over medical charge of L.D.R.E and cadre of 17 N.Fs.	[initials]

Army Form C.2118.

WAR DIARY
or
~~INTELLIGENCE SUMMARY.~~

(Erase heading not required.)

Instructions regarding War Diaries and Intelligence Summaries are contained in F. S. Regs., Part II. and the Staff Manual respectively. Title pages will be prepared in manuscript.

Hour, Date, Place	Summary of Events and Information	Remarks and References to Appendices
23/3/19	Numbers demobilized since 1st March R.Amb. 99 other ranks. Still to be demobilized. R.Amb. 106. RAS C. H.T have all been demobilized excepting 15 ORs in each F. Ambce. forming the Cadres.	[initials]
24/3/19.	Orders received from D D M S XXII Corps — No 1 C C S. Mons closed for admission of sick — C.C.S. in quarantine.	[initials]
SOIGNES. 25/3/19	A.D.M.S' Office opens 1100 Rue de la Station, SOIGNIES.	

(9 29 6) W 3332—1107 100,000 10/13 H W V Forms/C. 2118/10.

Army Form C. 2118.

Instructions regarding War Diaries and Intelligence Summaries are contained in F. S. Regs., Part II. and the Staff Manual respectively. Title pages will be prepared in manuscript.

WAR DIARY
or
~~INTELLIGENCE SUMMARY.~~
(*Erase heading not required.*)

Hour, Date, Place	Summary of Events and Information	Remarks and References to Appendices
25 3/19 (contd)	Captain A. D. DOWNES 1/1st Lowland Field Ambulance left for demobilisation	[initials]
	Received D.D.M.S. XXII Corps instructions to wire numbers releasable personnel surplus to Cadre, and period it will take to reduce Division to Cadre at present allotment	
	Replied 104 O.Rs. Period 35 days.	
26 3/19	Received D.D.M.S. XXII Corps Instruction – Restrictions No 1 C.C.S now off.	
	The following officers left to report to D.D.M.S., HAVRE	[initials]
	Captain C. H. K. SMITH, M.C. M.O. 1/4 K.O.S.B.	
	Captain . W. WEBB, M.O. 1/7 H.L.I.	
	Captain P. D. SCOTT M.O. 1/7 R.S.	

Army Form C. 2118.

Instructions regarding War Diaries and Intelligence Summaries are contained in F. S. Regs., Part II. and the Staff Manual respectively. Title pages will be prepared in manuscript.

WAR DIARY

~~or~~

~~INTELLIGENCE SUMMARY.~~

(Erase heading not required.)

Place	Date	Hour	Summary of Events and Information	Remarks and references to Appendices
		27 3/19	Staff A.D.M.S. Office sent down for demobilisation	
			Instructions issued to Field Ambulances that surplus vehicles should be returned to Ordnance. Ref Amendment No 3 Demobilisation Instructions France Part III	
		28 3/19	Instructions issued to 147 Bde RFA to return all RAMC personnel attached to 1/3rd Lowland Field Ambulance.	
			~~[illegible]~~ Captain (A/Lt Col) J. Young, DSO, O.C. 1/3rd Lowland Field Ambulance demobilised to be struck off the strength from 9-3-19. Authy D.G.M.S. No D.G. 208/7/199 d/23 3/19.	
			Captain D F BROWN, 1/3rd Lowland Field Ambulance posted to Labour Group, DOUAI.	
		29 3/19.	Nil	

D. D. & L., London, E.C. (A8001) Wt. W1771/M2031 750,000 5/17 Sch. 52 Forms/C2118/14

Instructions regarding War Diaries and Intelligence Summaries are contained in F. S. Regs., Part II. and the Staff Manual respectively. Title pages will be prepared in manuscript.

WAR DIARY

~~or~~

~~INTELLIGENCE SUMMARY.~~

(Erase heading not required.)

Army Form C. 2118.

Place	Date	Hour	Summary of Events and Information	Remarks and references to Appendices
	30	3/19	Received 52nd D H Q No A341 – Information required as to No. of Officers and Other Ranks entitled to demobilisation under A O 14 d/30-3-19. Numbers supplied Officers Nil Other Ranks 77 Instructions issued to Field Ambulances re men required for demobilisation who are attached to C C Ss to replace same by men from Cadres. These men to rejoin when Cadres entrain. Received 52nd D H Q No Q 133/20/8396 list of Units to entrain shortly for U K with equipment – Destination – GAILES, SCOTLAND. 3rd Lowland Field Ambulance included in list. 3rd Low. Fld Ambce, warned and DDMS XXII Corps advised.	[initials]

D. D. & L., London, E.C.
(A8004) Wt. W1771/M2031 750,000 5/17 Sch. 52 Forms/C2118/14

Army Form C. 2118.

Instructions regarding War Diaries and Intelligence Summaries are contained in F. S. Regs., Part II. and the Staff Manual respectively. Title pages will be prepared in manuscript.

WAR DIARY

~~or~~

~~INTELLIGENCE SUMMARY.~~

(Erase heading not required.)

Place	Date	Hour	Summary of Events and Information	Remarks and references to Appendices
	31/3/19		Received D.D.M.S. XXII Corps No B228. – All retainable men and volunteers for Army of Occupation to be sent to No 32 C.C.S. (VALENCIENNES) Fld. Ambces instructed accordingly. ~~Captain J C WILLIS, M.O.R.C., U.S.A. M.O. 1/6 H.L.I. left to report for duty 1st Army Musketry School~~	
SOIGNIES, BELGIUM 31-3-19.			A.D.M.S. 52nd (Lowland) Division A Y MacDougall [signature] Colonel, A.M.S.	

D. D. & L., London, E.C.
(A8001) Wt. W1771/M2031 750,000 5/17 Sch. 52 Forms/C2118/14

Appendix I

To:- No .... Rank.............. Name.................................

Unit.............................. 52nd (Lowland) Division.

Now that the time has come for you to leave the Army and go back to Civil Life, I wish, both personally and officially, to thank you for the service that you have given.

You take away with you the priceless knowledge that you have played a man's part in the Great War for Freedom and Fair Play.

You will take away with you also, your remembrance of your Comrades, your pride in your Field Ambulance, and your love for your Country.

You have played the Game; go on playing it and all will be well with the Great Empire which you have helped to save.

I wish you every prosperity and happiness.

Date..................

Lieut-General,

Commanding, XXII Corps.

Appendix II

R.1906/4

XXII CORPS.

First Army No. 111[illegible]/87 [illegible] 10/[illegible]/1919.

It has been noticed that nearly all the Deaths from Influenza recently have been among smaller Units, Army and Corps Troops etc., which have no Medical Officer of their own and which are not so well looked after with regard to ventilation, overcrowding, cleanliness of billets etc., Commanding Officers should pay particular attention to these points by frequent inspections.

It seems certain that poor ventilation and overcrowding by night is the chief reason why the disease spreads.

Further, it is important that men with Influenza should report sick and be sent to hospital early, otherwise their chances of recovering are greatly diminished.

Attention is drawn to A.R.O. [illegible] of [illegible]1/10/1918 and No. [illegible]14[illegible] of 5/11/1918.

Headquarters.
First Army.

(sgd) A.H. [illegible]. Capt.
for A.A.G. First Army.

All Formations & Units. [illegible].5[illegible]/4[illegible].

For information and necessary action.

A.G. Thomson

Headquarters.
14/[illegible]/1919.

[illegible]. COLONEL.
General Staff.
for [illegible] 22nd (Nov) [illegible].

All Formations & Units. [illegible].[illegible].[illegible],

The following wire from XXII Corps is published for information:-

"War Office telegram 7405 [illegible].D.[illegible] 10/[illegible]/1919 begins AAA Reference your C.R.[illegible]50 of 7th AAA Decided not to reintroduce compulsory vaccination at present AAA Attestation of volunteers should therefore proceed even if men refuse vaccination AAA Ends [illegible] of 15/[illegible]/19. cancelled AAA Addrd all concerned."

Appendix III

---

1. The Weekly Returns of Medical Officers in many cases shew very few men of their Units inspected.

Every man of each Unit should be medically inspected each week.

Medical Officers will arrange with Commanding Officers to inspect every man once a week and will report any difficulties to this Office

2. The numbers of SCABIES CASES still admitted is not creditable to the Division.

Some of these cases, which I have seen, state that they have suffered for 10 days before reporting Sick, which suggests that Medical Officers are not carrying out inspections in an efficient manner.

3. In future, on the admission of a Scabies Case the medical Officer will report to this Office through the Field Ambulance concerned whether the case was discovered at an Inspection or whether the man reported Sick on his own initiative. If the latter the medical officer will report when he inspected the man last and the reason for not having inspected him within the preceding 8 days if such is the case.

4. Certain medical officers still report the presence of lice in their units, though to a small extent. Such medical Officers will advise their Commanding Officers in the matter and will make every endeavour to completely eradicate LICE.

A. J. MacDougall

11th March, 1919. Colonel. A.M.S.

A. D. M. S. 52nd (Lowland) Division.

April 1919

CONFIDENTIAL

WAR DIARY 140/3552 VR 13

of

A.D.M.S. 52nd (Lowland) Division

From 1st April 1919 to 30th April 1919

Volume (2.)

Sheet No. 1

Instructions regarding War Diaries and Intelligence Summaries are contained in F. S. Regs., Part II. and the Staff Manual respectively. Title pages will be prepared in manuscript.

WAR DIARY
or
~~INTELLIGENCE SUMMARY~~.
(Erase heading not required.)

Army Form C. 2118.

Place	Date	Hour	Summary of Events and Information	Remarks and references to Appendices
SOIGNIES	1/4/19		Nil RW	
BELGIUM	2/4/19		Nil RW	
"	3/4/19		Captain J. E. EVANS, RAMC(TC) / Lieut. J. K. K. GUTHRIE, M.O.R.C., U.S.A. } Posted to No 30 C.C.S. LALOUVIERE RW	
	4/4/19		Field Ambulance Quartermasters detailed to inspect Medical Equipment of all Units and indent to complete to Establishment where necessary RW	
	5/4/19		Nil RW	
	6/4/19		Colonel A. J. MACDOUGALL C.M.G. R.A.M.C. assumed duties of A.D.M.S. Mons Cadres. RW	
	7/4/19		Field Ambulances instructed to render a certificate, prior to entrainment of Cadres that all medical and Surgical Equipment, (including Drugs), surplus to RW	

A6945 Wt. W11422/M1160 350,000 12/16 D. D. & L. Forms/C./2118/14.

Sheet No 2.

WAR DIARY
or
~~INTELLIGENCE SUMMARY.~~
(Erase heading not required.)

Army Form C. 2118.

Instructions regarding War Diaries and Intelligence Summaries are contained in F. S. Regs., Part II, and the Staff Manual respectively. Title pages will be prepared in manuscript.

Place	Date	Hour	Summary of Events and Information	Remarks and references to Appendices
SOIGNIES	7/4/19		continued	
			— to establishment had been returned to No 19	
			Advanced Depot Medical Stores	RW
"	8/4/19		Nil	RW
	9/4/19		Nil	RW
	10/4/19		Nil	RW
	11/4/19		Nil	RW
	12/4/19		Nil	RW
	13/4/19		Nil	RW
	14/4/19		Nil	RW
	15/4/19		Nil	RW
	16/4/19		Nil	RW
	17/4/19		Nil	RW
	18/4/19		Demobilisation for Field Ambulances now completed,	
			only Cadres remaining	RW
	19/4/19		Nil	RW

A6945 Wt. W11422/M1160 350,000 12/16 D. D. & L. Forms/C./2118/14.

Sheet No 3.

Instructions regarding War Diaries and Intelligence Summaries are contained in F. S. Regs., Part II. and the Staff Manual respectively. Title pages will be prepared in manuscript.

WAR DIARY
or
~~INTELLIGENCE SUMMARY~~.
(*Erase heading not required.*)

Army Form C. 2118.

Place	Date	Hour	Summary of Events and Information	Remarks and references to Appendices
SOIGNIES	20/4/19		Nil. RW	
	21/4/19		All motor cycles returned to M.T. Park Mons. RW	
	22/4/19		Nil RW	
	23/4/19		Received 52 Division Q 535 d/23-4-19 – Division to commence entraining on 27/4/19. RW	
	24/4/19		Nil RW	
	25/4/19		Received 52nd Division Q 235/7 d/24-4-19 forecasts of moves for 27th, 28th and 29th. – No RAMC included. RW	
	26/4/19		Nil RW	
	27/4/19		Departures of cadres detailed for 27th RW	
	28/4/19		-do- " " 28th RW	
	29/4/19		-do- " " 29th RW	
	30/4/19		Nil. RW	

M Walker Major,
for Colonel,
A.M.S.
A.D.M.S. 52nd (Lowland) Division

A6945 Wt. W11422/M1160 350,000 12/16 D. D. & L. Forms/C./2118/14.

Instructions regarding War Diaries and Intelligence Summaries are contained in F. S. Regs., Part II. and the Staff Manual respectively. Title pages will be prepared in manuscript.

Sheet No I

Army Form C. 2118.

WAR DIARY
or
~~INTELLIGENCE~~ SUMMARY.
(*Erase heading not required.*)

Place	Date	Hour	Summary of Events and Information	Remarks and references to Appendices
Soignies	May 1		Nil	RW
	2		Nil	RW
	3		Instructions received to reduce Cadres of Field Ambulances to 1 Officer 44 ORs instead of 2 Officers 44 ORs	RW
	4		Nil	RW
	5		Nil	RW
	6		Nil	RW
	7		Captain J.P. Quinn RAMC M.C to be struck of the strength of his Unit on the expiration of his leave from U.K. Authority DMS No 98/134 dated 2-5-19.	RW
	8		All imprest accounts being closed arrangements were made for personnel of Field Ambulances of this Divn to be attached to a neighbouring Unit for pay. RAMC personnel attached to 1/6 Btn 1/5 R.S.F. for pay.	RW RW
	9.		All Medical Officers to be struck off the strength of their Units and to be taken on strength of No 1 Area	RW

A6945 Wt. W11422/M1160 350,000 12/16 D. D. & L. Forms/C./2118/14.

Instructions regarding War Diaries and Intelligence Summaries are contained in F. S. Regs., Part II. and the Staff Manual respectively. Title pages will be prepared in manuscript.

Army Form C. 2118.

WAR DIARY
or
~~INTELLIGENCE SUMMARY~~.
(Erase heading not required.)

Sheet 2

Place	Date	Hour	Summary of Events and Information	Remarks and references to Appendices
Soyrmes	May 9		and are available for reposting as required. Authority DAG. No CR 3172/Med	
			At this time the Quartermaster of the 1/2nd Lowland Field Ambulance being on leave to U.K. Capt A/Major Black CSP. continues to command the Cadre of that Unit	RW
	10		Nil	RW
	11		Nil	RW
	12		Nil	RW
	13		Capt A/Major Walker R.G. RAMC. M.C is struck off the strength of his Unit 1/3rd Lowland Field Ambulance, and relinquishes the acting rank of Major on being taken on the strength of No 1 Area.	
			Capt Lennie RAMC O.C 1/1st Lowland Field Ambulance handed over the command of his unit to the Quartermaster and was himself taken on the strength of No 1 Area.	RW

A6945 Wt. W11422/M1160 350,000 12/16 D. D. & L. Forms/C./2118/14.

Army Form C. 2118.

WAR DIARY
or
~~INTELLIGENCE SUMMARY~~.
(Erase heading not required.)

Instructions regarding War Diaries and Intelligence Summaries are contained in F. S. Regs., Part II. and the Staff Manual respectively. Title pages will be prepared in manuscript.

Sheet No 3

Place	Date	Hour	Summary of Events and Information	Remarks and references to Appendices
Soignies	May 14		Nil	RW
	15		Nil	RW
	16		Nil	RW
	17		Nil	RW
	18		Nil	RW
	19		Nil	RW
	20		Nil	RW
	21		Nil	RW
	22		Nil.	RW
	23		Instructions received from ADMS. Mons Cadres to demobilise all RAMC personnel who enlisted in 1914	RW
	24		40 O.R. RAMC leave Field Ambulances of the Division for Concentration Camp.	RW
	25		Lieut and. Qr Mr Liddell 1/2 Lowland Field Ambulance returned from leave to U.K	RW

A6945 Wt. W11422/M1160 350,000 12/16 D. D. & L. Forms/C./2118/14.

Instructions regarding War Diaries and Intelligence Summaries are contained in F. S. Regs., Part II. and the Staff Manual respectively. Title pages will be prepared in manuscript.

Army Form C. 2118.

WAR DIARY
or
~~INTELLIGENCE SUMMARY.~~
(Erase heading not required.)

Sheet No 4

Place	Date	Hour	Summary of Events and Information	Remarks and references to Appendices
Soignies	May 26		Capt T/Major Black C.S.P. RAMC M.C handed over the command 1/2 Lowland Field Ambulance to Lieut and Qr Mr. Liddell and relinquished the acting rank of Major on being taken on the strength of No 1 Area.	RW
	May 27		Nil	RW
	28		Nil	RW
	29		Nil	RW
	30		Nil	RW
	31		The 1/5 Battn RSF having entrained for embarkation to U.K. the personnel of Field Ambulances of this Division are attached for pay to C.R.E. 52nd Divn	RW

R J Walker Capt RAMC MC
[illegible] 52 Low Division

A6945 Wt. W11422/M1160 350,000 12/16 D. D. & L. Forms/C./2118/14.

Army Form A. 2007.

CENTRAL REGISTRY.

Central Registry No. and Date.	Attached Files.

SUBJECT, AND OFFICE OF ORIGIN.

Referred to	Date	Referred to	Date	Referred to	Date
				P. A.	Date

Schedule of Correspondence.

(6411) W 2862/P1290 1,500,000 6/18 McA & W Ltd. (E 3389)

A.F. C.2118.

WAR DIARY.

JUNE 1919

52.

A. D. M. S. ^ LOWLAND DIVISION.

June 1919

Instructions regarding War Diaries and Intelligence Summaries are contained in F. S. Regs., Part II. and the Staff Manual respectively. Title pages will be prepared in manuscript.

1

WAR DIARY
or
INTELLIGENCE SUMMARY.
(Erase heading not required.)

Army Form C. 2118.

1919

A.D.M.S.
Lowland Div

1.

Place	Date	Hour	Summary of Events and Information	Remarks and references to Appendices
	JUNE			
OHLIGS	1		Very fine weather. Wrote monthly Sanitary Report for May.	WWolsey Col
	2		Conference D.M.S. at 64 CCS. All D.A.D.M.S. A.DsM.S. and F.A. Commanders present	OE
	4		Threatening weather. G.O.C. sent to 36 C.C.S. for "X" ray of his Elbow injured yesterday while playing tennis. Report no fracture. D.A.D.M.S. accompanied him to C.C.S. Went round Sanitary inspection taking O.C. 81 San Sect showing him the defects in OHLIGS &c.	OE
			Maj RANKINE returned from leave. Rain all night.	
	5.		Still raining. San Inspn of OHLIGS continued. 5/6 R. Scots billets inspected with G.O.C. No 2 Lowland BDE + O.C. (Lt COL MUDIE) Inspection of D.H.Q. with D.A.D.M.S. G.O.C. taken to No 3 G.H. for massage.	OE
	7.		Saw G.O.C. c D.A.D.M.S. and recommended another "X" ray at 36 C.C.S. this was done. No fracture reported.	
	9		Cancelled RHINE TRIP for 11 R. Scots owing to reported case of Scarlet fever in billeting area (vicinity)	OE
	10		Capt CUNNINGHAM R.A.M.C. arrived for duty + posted to 2/1 F.A. Investigated + visited reputed case of Scarlet fever at HAAN - it is not Scarlet fever + troops are not near. Inspected 2nd Lowland BDE School. Inspected 16th H.L.I.	OE
	11.		Lt COL BRUCE 2/1st E.L. F.A. ordered to 9 C.C.S. BONN. Maj RANKINE (D.A.D.M.S.) left for U.K. on demobilization. Capt CROLY assumes these duties for the present. Inspected meat protection arrangements in HILDEN + OHLIGS (refilling points)	OE

D. D. & L., London, E.C. (A8001) Wt. W1771/M2031 750,000 5/17 Sch. 52 Forms/C2118/14

Instructions regarding War Diaries and Intelligence Summaries are contained in F. S. Regs., Part II. and the Staff Manual respectively. Title pages will be prepared in manuscript.

3

WAR DIARY
or
INTELLIGENCE SUMMARY.
(Erase heading not required.)

Army Form C. 2118.

1919

A.D.M.S.
LOWLAND DIV

2.

Place	Date	Hour	Summary of Events and Information	Remarks and references to Appendices
	JUNE			
OHLIGS.	11	2 pm	Inspected Infantry attached for R.A.M.C. Duties to 27/F.A. – a good lot but poor physique.	OC
	12		Took O.C. (81 San Sect) round various units to familiarize him with conditions prevailing in Cookhouses, dining rooms etc of 1/4 R.S.F. (HILDEN)	OC
	13.		Inspn of 50th BDE R.F.A. Report sent in.	OC
			Inspected refilling point No 1 Lowld BDE (105 Co R.A.S.C.) + 16th H.L.I. at LANDWEHR + WIESCHEID – also billets in these localities.	OC
	14		Threatening morning clearing later. D.D.M.S. II Corps called and visited our Skin hospital.	
			GENL BUTLER handed over command of Lowland Div to GENL TUDOR who commanded the 9th Div formerly.	OC
	15		LT WALLACE R.F.A. reported for examination + was evacuated as he was suffering from severe VARIX in both legs.	
	16.		Inspected at 5/6 Royal Scots (OHLIGS).	
			Investigated case of Typhoid (PLÜMACHER – KONIGSTR. WEYER) Officer billeted there has left + was re-inoculated + in quarantine as contact	
			Visited prisoners in cells in STADHAUS – SOLINGEN + sent in report to No 1 L. BDE.	
			Called at BDE H.Q. re same matter.	
	17.		J–3 day very hot weather. Issued Medical arrangements in connection with the moves forward into Germany	App II
			Visited No 2 Lowld BDE + outpost 6 K.O.S.B. (KLUSE POST).	
			Visited 28/F.A. re march on J-1 + handing over etc.	OC

D. D. & L., London, E.C. (A8003) Wt. W1771/M2031 750,000 5/17 Sch. 52 Forms/C2118/14

Instructions regarding War Diaries and Intelligence Summaries are contained in F. S. Regs., Part II. and the Staff Manual respectively. Title pages will be prepared in manuscript.

3

WAR DIARY
or
~~INTELLIGENCE SUMMARY.~~
(Erase heading not required.)

1919

Army Form C. 2118.

A.D.M.S.
LOWLAND DIV

Place	Date	Hour	Summary of Events and Information 3	Remarks and references to Appendices
OHLIGS	JUNE 18		"J – 2" day Visited "B" Sect 27/F.A. "B" 51/R.F.A. also saw C.R.A. re Venereal Disease. He is taking the question up among officers more strongly. Visited 9th M.G.C. and arranged for their M.O. (LT GRANT) to proceed to 16th H.L.I. until arrival of Capt GEE off leave. He is then to join 27/F.A. for the march into GERMANY. LT GRANT proceeds to C.M. tomorrow therefore Capt TODD must proceed with 16th H.L.I. and return on completion	OE
	19		J–1 Day Very hot day. No 1 Lowland BDE moved forward according to plan. B.H.Q. near KLUSE POST GRAFRATH. 28th F.A. to WALD-CENTRALE Sheet CÖLN 59 E 3.05–30. And only one battn left in SOLINGEN viz 51st H.L.I. The HIGHLAND DIV arrived overnight & took over billets vacated by 1st LOWLAND BDE. The 2/3 W.R. F.A. took over from 28/F.A. Visited all units in new area, as also those in HAAN.	OE
	20		Visited & inspected 27/F.A. Heat very great. Capt McCORMACK & LT WHITFIELD RAMC arrived for duty to liberate 2 officers ordered to India (Capts PATERSON & STEWART)	OE
	21.		STADTBAUMEISTER HAPPE called re sanitation of OHLIGS – I gave him my views and instructions as to remedy of certain defects. Visited 28/F.A. at CENTRAL. 51st H.L.I. moved out from SOLINGEN to OBERSCHEIDT, STÖCKER & DEMMART.	OE
	22		Fine & cool. Interview with G.O.C. Capts PATERSON & STEWART leave for U.K. for transfer to INDIA sailing on 24th.	

D. D. & L., London, E.C. (A8001) Wt. W1771/M2031 750,000 5/17 Sch. 52 Forms C2118/14

Instructions regarding War Diaries and Intelligence Summaries are contained in F. S. Regs., Part II, and the Staff Manual respectively. Title pages will be prepared in manuscript.

4.

WAR DIARY
or
INTELLIGENCE SUMMARY.
(Erase heading not required.)

Army Form C. 2118.

1919

A.D.M.S
LOWLAND DIV

4.

Place	Date JUNE	Hour	Summary of Events and Information	Remarks and references to Appendices
OHLIGS	23		Much cooler. Orders received re moves forward if Peace not signed by 7.p.m tonight. All officers to remain with their units etc. Visited 28th + 27th F.A — all prepared for advance at or after 03.00 hrs on 24th.	OE
	24		Heavy rain + much wind all day + colder. The mark has again fallen — 10 marks = 2/9 instead of 3/3. Office routine.	OE
	25		Cool but fine. Visited transport lines 10th H.L.I. + 11th R. Scots at HAAN + H.Q. 5th M.G.C. Heavy rain at night.	OE
	26		Orders received from Corps to hand over duties of A.D.M.S. to Lt Col H.G. MARTIN C.M.G. + on relief to take over command of No 47 GENERAL HOSPITAL — BONN. Visited 27th + 28th F.As.	OE
	27		Very wet + stormy. Went round 3rd Lowland BDE. Saw G.O.C. + all unit commanders.	OE
"	30		Arrived from 47 General Hospital in relief of Colonel O.W. Elsner. Assumed duties ~~from~~ 1.7.19 inclusive H.G. Martin Lt Col RAMC	

D. D. & L., London, E.C.
(A8001) Wt. W1771/M2031 750,000 5/17 Sch. 52 Forms/C2118/14

LOWLAND DIVISION. App II SECRET.

MEDICAL ARRANGEMENTS. No 3

The following will be the distribution of Medical Officers for the march:-

1st LOWLAND BRIGADE GROUP.

1/5 K.O.S.B.	Captain R.CUNNINGHAM,	R.A.M.C.
15th H.L.I.	Captain M.C.PATERSON,M.C;	R.A.M.C.
51st H.L.I.	Captain W.DUGUID.	R.A.M.C.
28th Field Ambulance.		
	Lt.Col. C.M.DREW,D.S.O.	R.A.M.C.
	* Captain W.A.TODD.	R.A.M.C.

* Available if necessary for other Units in BRIGADE requiring medical assistance.

2nd LOWLAND BRIGADE GROUP.

5/6th R. S.	Captain P.A.STEWART,	R.A.M.C.
11th R. S.	Captain D.CRELLIN, M.C.	R.A.M.C.
6th K.O.S.B.	Captain J.CHARNLEY,	R.A.M.C.
27th Field Ambulance.		
	Lt.Col. J.M.A.COSTELLO, M.C.	R.A.M.C.

3rd LOWLAND BRIGADE GROUP.

1/4th R.S.F.	Captain G.G.OLD,	R.A.M.C.
1/8th S. R.	Captain A.B.BROOK,	R.A.M.C.
9th S. R.	Captain E.C.TAMPLIN,	R.A.M.C.
"B" Section, 27th F. A.		
	Major J.R.N.WARBURTON, M.C.	R.A.M.C.

LOWLAND D.H.Q. GROUP.

Lowland Div:Arty:	Captain J.McCULLOCH,	R.A.M.C.
Lowland D.A.C.	Captain C.E.WILMOT.	R.A.M.C.
16th H.L.I.	* Lt:A.B.GRANT (M.O.i/c 9th M.G.B.)	

*Should join before "J"day pending arrival of Capt:A.O.GEE from leave. On relief (if before "J" day) Lt.GRANT will join 27th F.A. H.Q. with 2nd LOWLAND BRIGADE GROUP.

50th Bde. R.F.A.(less one battery)	Captain J.McCULLOCH,	R.A.M.C.
51st Bde. R.F.A.(less ~~one~~ two battery)		
LOWLAND D.A.C.	Captain C.E.WILMOT.	R.A.M.C.

If these Units march together one M.O. should suffice thus liberating one for duty with 27th F.A. H.Q. if required.

6 M.A.C. Cars arrive on "J"-2 day and will be distributed 2 to each F.A. & 2 to HILDEN for evacuation of sick to C.C.S. when necessary.

F.A.Commanders 1. Will chose suitable buildings for temporary hospitals en route & R.M.Os. will keep in touch with them re disposal of any sick who require transport or evacuation.

2. Will furnish a "daily state & "Situation report" to this Office by 18.00 hours daily.

3. Attention is directed to Lowland Div:R.A.M.C.Order No.2.

A.D.M.S.Office closes at HACKHAUS & opens at GRAFRATH on "J"day at an hour to be notified later.

Acknowledge (F.As.only).

Lowland Division H.Q.
17/6/1919.
990/10/2.

D W Arnance Colonel.
A.D.M.S., Lowland Divn:

DISTRIBUTION:-

1. D.M.S., Rhine Army.
2. D.D.M.S.,11 Corps.
3. Lowland "G".
4. Lowland "A".
5. Lowland "Q".
6. No.1 Lowland Brigade.
7. No.2 Lowland Brigade.
8. No.3 Lowland Brigade.
9. M.G.B.
10. 16th H.L.I.
11 - 13 Field Ambulances.
14. C.R.E.
15. C.R.A.
16. Lowland Division Train.
17. Signals.
18. D.A.D.O.S.
19. D.A.D.V.S.
20 - 34 R.M.Os.
Diary (2)
File.

www.ingramcontent.com/pod-product-compliance
Lightning Source LLC
Chambersburg PA
CBHW081400160426
43193CB00013B/2072
* 9 7 8 1 4 7 4 5 2 8 9 4 8 *